D1557552

Collected
Black Women's
Poetry

THE SCHOMBURG LIBRARY OF
NINETEENTH-CENTURY BLACK WOMEN WRITERS

General Editor, Henry Louis Gates, Jr.

Titles are listed chronologically; collections that include works published over a span of years are listed according to the publication date of their initial work.

Collected
Black Women's Poetry

Volume 1

Edited by
JOAN R. SHERMAN

New York   Oxford
OXFORD UNIVERSITY PRESS
1988

Oxford University Press

Oxford   New York   Toronto
Delhi   Bombay   Calcutta   Madras   Karachi
Petaling Jaya   Singapore   Hong Kong   Tokyo
Nairobi   Dar es Salaam   Cape Town
Melbourne   Auckland

and associated companies in
Beirut   Berlin   Ibadan   Nicosia

Library of Congress Cataloging-in-Publication Data

Collected black women's poetry.
(The Schomburg library of nineteenth-century black
women writers)
1. American poetry—Afro-American authors.
2. American poetry—Women authors.   3. American
poetry—19th century.   4. Afro-American women—
Poetry.   I. Sherman, Joan Rita.   II. Series.
PS591.N4C57   1988   811'.008'09287   87-20379
ISBN 0-19-505253-6 (v. 1)
ISBN 0-19-505267-6 (set)

2 4 6 8 10 9 7 5 3

Printed in the United States of America
on acid-free paper

The
Schomburg Library
of
Nineteenth-Century
Black Women Writers
is
Dedicated
in Memory
of
PAULINE AUGUSTA COLEMAN GATES

1916–1987

PUBLISHER'S NOTE

FOREWORD
In Her Own Write

Henry Louis Gates, Jr.

One muffled strain in the Silent South, a jarring chord and a vague and uncomprehended cadenza has been and still is the Negro. And of that muffled chord, the one mute and voiceless note has been the sadly expectant Black Woman, ...

The "other side" has not been represented by one who "lives there." And not many can more sensibly realize and more accurately tell the weight and the fret of the "long dull pain" than the open-eyed but hitherto voiceless Black Woman of America.

. . . as our Caucasian barristers are not to blame if they cannot *quite* put themselves in the dark man's place, neither should the dark man be wholly expected fully and adequately to reproduce the exact Voice of the Black Woman.

—ANNA JULIA COOPER, *A Voice From the South* (1892)

The birth of the Afro-American literary tradition occurred in 1773, when Phillis Wheatley published a book of poetry. Despite the fact that her book garnered for her a remarkable amount of attention, Wheatley's journey to the printer had been a most arduous one. Sometime in 1772, a young African girl walked demurely into a room in Boston to undergo an oral examination, the results of which would determine the direction of her life and work. Perhaps she was shocked upon entering the appointed room. For there, perhaps gathered in a semicircle, sat eighteen of Boston's most notable citizens. Among them were John Erving, a prominent Boston merchant; the Reverend Charles Chauncy, pastor of the Tenth Congregational Church; and John Hancock, who would later gain fame for his signature on the Declaration of Independence. At the center of this group was His Excellency, Thomas Hutchinson, governor of Massachusetts, with Andrew Oliver, his lieutenant governor, close by his side.

Why had this august group been assembled? Why had it seen fit to summon this young African girl, scarcely eighteen years old, before it? This group of "the most respectable Characters in *Boston*," as it would later define itself, had assembled to question closely the African adolescent on the slender sheaf of poems that she claimed to have "written by herself." We can only speculate on the nature of the questions posed to the fledgling poet. Perhaps they asked her to identify and explain—for all to hear—exactly who were the Greek and Latin gods and poets alluded to so frequently in her work. Perhaps they asked her to conjugate a verb in Latin or even to translate randomly selected passages from the Latin, which she and her master, John Wheatley, claimed that she "had made some Progress in." Or perhaps they asked her to recite from memory key passages from the texts of John Milton and Alexander Pope, the two poets by whom the African claimed to be most directly influenced. We do not know.

We do know, however, that the African poet's responses were more than sufficient to prompt the eighteen august gentlemen to compose, sign, and publish a two-paragraph "Attestation," an open letter "To the Publick" that prefaces Phillis Wheatley's book and that reads in part:

> We whose Names are under-written, do assure the World, that the Poems specified in the following Page, were (as we

verily believe) written by Phillis, a young Negro Girl, who was but a few Years since, brought an uncultivated Barbarian from *Africa,* and has ever since been, and now is, under the Disadvantage of serving as a Slave in a Family in this Town. She has been examined by some of the best Judges, and is thought qualified to write them.

So important was this document in securing a publisher for Wheatley's poems that it forms the signal element in the prefatory matter preceding her *Poems on Various Subjects, Religious and Moral,* published in London in 1773.

Without the published "Attestation," Wheatley's publisher claimed, few would believe that an African could possibly have written poetry all by herself. As the eighteen put the matter clearly in their letter, "Numbers would be ready to suspect they were not really the Writings of Phillis." Wheatley and her master, John Wheatley, had attempted to publish a similar volume in 1772 in Boston, but Boston publishers had been incredulous. One year later, "Attestation" in hand, Phillis Wheatley and her master's son, Nathaniel Wheatley, sailed for England, where they completed arrangements for the publication of a volume of her poems with the aid of the Countess of Huntington and the Earl of Dartmouth.

This curious anecdote, surely one of the oddest oral examinations on record, is only a tiny part of a larger, and even more curious, episode in the Enlightenment. Since the beginning of the sixteenth century, Europeans had wondered aloud whether or not the African "species of men," as they were most commonly called, *could* ever create formal literature, could ever master "the arts and sciences." If they could, the argument ran, then the African variety of humanity was fundamentally related to the European variety. If not, then it seemed clear that the African was destined by nature

to be a slave. This was the burden shouldered by Phillis
Wheatley when she successfully defended herself and the au-
thorship of her book against counterclaims and doubts.

Indeed, with her successful defense, Wheatley launched
two traditions at once—the black American literary tradition
and the black woman's literary tradition. If it is extraordinary
that not just one but both of these traditions were founded
simultaneously by a black woman—certainly an event unique
in the history of literature—it is also ironic that this important fact of common, coterminous literary origins seems to
have escaped most scholars.

That the progenitor of the black literary tradition was a
woman means, in the most strictly literal sense, that all sub-
sequent black writers have evolved in a matrilinear line of
descent, and that each, consciously or unconsciously, has extended and revised a canon whose foundation was the poetry
of a black woman. Early black writers seem to have been
keenly aware of Wheatley's founding role, even if most of
her white reviewers were more concerned with the implica-
tions of her race than her gender. Jupiter Hammon, for example, whose 1760 broadside "An Evening Thought. Sal-
vation by Christ, With Penitential Cries" was the first
individual poem published by a black American, acknowl-
edged Wheatley's influence by selecting her as the subject of
his second broadside, "An Address to Miss Phillis Wheatly
[*sic*], Ethiopian Poetess, in Boston," which was published at
Hartford in 1778. And George Moses Horton, the second
Afro-American to publish a book of poetry in English (1829),
brought out in 1838 an edition of his *Poems By A Slave*
bound together with Wheatley's work. Indeed, for fifty-six
years, between 1773 and 1829, when Horton published *The
Hope of Liberty*, Wheatley was the *only* black person to have
published a book of imaginative literature in English. So

central was this black woman's role in the shaping of the Afro-American literary tradition that, as one historian has maintained, the history of the reception of Phillis Wheatley's poetry *is* the history of Afro-American literary criticism. Well into the nineteenth century, Wheatley and the black literary tradition were the same entity.

But Wheatley is not the only black woman writer who stands as a pioneering figure in Afro-American literature. Just as Wheatley gave birth to the genre of black poetry, Ann Plato was the first Afro-American to publish a book of essays (1841) and Harriet E. Wilson was the first black person to publish a novel in the United States (1859).

Despite this pioneering role of black women in the tradition, however, many of their contributions before this century have been all but lost or unrecognized. As Hortense Spillers observed as recently as 1983,

> With the exception of a handful of autobiographical narratives from the nineteenth century, the black woman's realities are virtually suppressed until the period of the Harlem Renaissance and later. Essentially the black woman as artist, as intellectual spokesperson for her own cultural apprenticeship, has not existed before, for anyone. At the source of [their] own symbol-making task, [the community of black women writers] confronts, therefore, a tradition of work that is quite recent, its continuities, broken and sporadic.

Until now, it has been extraordinarily difficult to establish the formal connections between early black women's writing and that of the present, precisely because our knowledge of their work has been broken and sporadic. Phillis Wheatley, for example, while certainly the most reprinted and discussed poet in the tradition, is also one of the least understood. Ann Plato's seminal work, *Essays* (which includes biographies and poems), has not been reprinted since it was published a century and a half ago. And Harriet Wilson's *Our Nig,* her compelling novel of a black woman's expanding conscious- ness in a racist Northern antebellum environment, never re- ceived even *one* review or comment at a time when virtually *all* works written by black people were heralded by abolition- ists as salient arguments against the existence of human slav- ery. Many of the books reprinted in this set experienced a similar fate, the most dreadful fate for an author: that of being ignored then relegated to the obscurity of the rare book section of a university library. We can only wonder how many other texts in the black woman's tradition have been lost to this generation of readers or remain unclassified or uncatalogued and, hence, unread.

This was not always so, however. Black women writers dominated the final decade of the nineteenth century, perhaps spurred to publish by an 1886 essay entitled "The Coming American Novelist," which was published in *Lippincott's Monthly Magazine* and written by "A Lady From Philadel- phia." This pseudonymous essay argued that the "Great American Novel" would be written by a black person. Her argument is so curious that it deserves to be repeated:

> When we come to formulate our demands of the Coming American Novelist, we will agree that he must be native- born. His ancestors may come from where they will, but we must give him a birthplace and have the raising of him. Still, the longer his family has been here the better he will represent us. Suppose he should have no country but ours, no traditions but those he has learned here, no longings apart from us, no future except in our future—the orphan of the world, he finds with us his home. And with all this, suppose he refuses to be fused into that grand conglomerate we call the "Amer- ican type." With us, he is not of us. He is original, he has humor, he is tender, he is passive and fiery, he has been

taught what we call justice, and he has his own opinion about
it. He has suffered everything a poet, a dramatist, a novelist
need suffer before he comes to have his lips anointed. And
with it all he is in one sense a spectator, a little out of the
race. How would these conditions go towards forming an
original development? In a word, suppose the coming novelist
is of African origin? When one comes to consider the subject,
there is no improbability in it. One thing is certain,—our
great novel will not be written by the typical American.

An atypical American, indeed. Not only would the great
American novel be written by an African-American, it would
be written by an African-American *woman:*

Yet farther: I have used the generic masculine pronoun
because it is convenient; but Fate keeps revenge in store. It
was a woman who, taking the wrongs of the African as her
theme, wrote the novel that awakened the world to their
reality, and why should not the coming novelist be a woman
as well as an African? She—the woman of that race—has
some claims on Fate which are not yet paid up.

It is these claims on fate that we seek to pay by publishing
The Schomburg Library of Nineteenth-Century Black Women
Writers.

This theme would be repeated by several black women
authors, most notably by Anna Julia Cooper, a prototypical
black feminist whose 1892 *A Voice From the South* can be
considered to be one of the original texts of the black feminist movement. It was Cooper who first analyzed the fal-
lacy of referring to "the Black man" when speaking of black
people and who argued that just as white men cannot speak
through the consciousness of black men, neither can black
men "fully and adequately . . . reproduce the exact Voice of
the Black Woman." Gender and race, she argues, cannot be

conflated, except in the instance of a black woman's voice, and it is this voice which must be uttered and to which we must listen. As Cooper puts the matter so compellingly:

> It is not the intelligent woman vs. the ignorant woman; nor the white woman vs. the black, the brown, and the red,—it is not even the cause of woman vs. man. Nay, 'tis woman's strongest vindication for speaking that *the world needs to hear her voice*. It would be subversive of every human interest that the cry of one-half the human family be stifled. Woman in stepping from the pedestal of statue-like inactivity in the domestic shrine, and daring to think and move and speak,—to undertake to help shape, mold, and direct the thought of her age, is merely completing the circle of the world's vision. Hers is every interest that has lacked an interpreter and a defender. Her cause is linked with that of every agony that has been dumb—every wrong that needs a voice.
>
> It is no fault of man's that he has not been able to see truth from her standpoint. It does credit both to his head and heart that no greater mistakes have been committed or even wrongs perpetrated while she sat making tatting and snipping paper flowers. Man's own innate chivalry and the mutual interdependence of their interests have insured his treating her cause, in the main at least, as his own. And he is pardonably surprised and even a little chagrined, perhaps, to find his legislation not considered "perfectly lovely" in every respect. But in any case his work is only impoverished by her remaining dumb. The world has had to limp along with the wobbling gait and one-sided hesitancy of a man with one eye. Suddenly the bandage is removed from the other eye and the whole body is filled with light. It sees a circle where before it saw a segment. The darkened eye restored, every member rejoices with it.

The myopic sight of the darkened eye can only be restored when the full range of the black woman's voice, with its own special timbres and shadings, remains mute no longer.

Similarly, Victoria Earle Matthews, an author of short stories and essays, and a cofounder in 1896 of the National Association of Colored Women, wrote in her stunning essay, "The Value of Race Literature" (1895), that "when the literature of our race is developed, it will of necessity be different in all essential points of greatness, true heroism and real Christianity from what we may at the present time, for convenience, call American literature." Matthews argued that this great tradition of Afro-American literature would be the textual outlet "for the unnaturally suppressed inner lives which our people have been compelled to lead." Once these "unnaturally suppressed inner lives" of black people are unveiled, no "grander diffusion of mental light" will shine more brightly, she concludes, than that of the articulate Afro-American woman:

And now comes the question, What part shall we women play in the Race Literature of the future? . . . within the compass of one small journal ["Woman's Era"] we have struck out a new line of departure—a journal, a record of Race interests gathered from all parts of the United States, carefully selected, moistened, winnowed and garnered by the ablest intellects of educated colored women, shrinking at no lofty theme, shirking no serious duty, aiming at every possible excellence, and determined to do their part in the future uplifting of the race.

If twenty women, by their concentrated efforts in one literary movement, can meet with such success as has engendered, planned out, and so successfully consummated this convention, what much more glorious results, what wider spread success, what grander diffusion of mental light will not come forth at the bidding of the enlarged hosts of women writers, already called into being by the stimulus of your efforts?

And here let me speak one word for my journalistic sisters

who have already entered the broad arena of journalism.
Before the "Woman's Era" had come into existence, no one
except themselves can appreciate the bitter experience and
sore disappointments under which they have at all times been
compelled to pursue their chosen vocations.

If their brothers of the press have had their difficulties to
contend with, I am here as a sister journalist to state, from
the fullness of knowledge, that their task has been an easy
one compared with that of the colored woman in journalism.

Woman's part in Race Literature, as in Race building, is
the most important part and has been so in all ages. . . . All
through the most remote epochs she has done her share in
literature. . . .

One of the most important aspects of this set is the repub-
lication of the salient texts from 1890 to 1910, which literary
historians could well call "The Black Woman's Era." In addition to Mary Helen Washington's definitive edition of
Cooper's *A Voice From the South*, we have reprinted two novels by Amelia Johnson, Frances Harper's *Iola Leroy*, two
novels by Emma Dunham Kelley, Alice Dunbar-Nelson's two
impressive collections of short stories, and Pauline Hopkins's
three serialized novels as well as her monumental novel,
Contending Forces—all published between 1890 and 1910. Indeed, black women published more works of fiction in these
two decades than black men had published in the previous
half century. Nevertheless, this great achievement has been
ignored.

Moreover, the writings of nineteenth-century Afro-
American women in general have remained buried in obscurity, accessible only in research libraries or in overpriced and
poorly edited reprints. Many of these books have never been
reprinted at all; in some instances only one or two copies are
extant. In these works of fiction, poetry, autobiography, bi-

ography, essays, and journalism resides the mind of the nineteenth-century Afro-American woman. Until these works are made readily available to teachers and their students, a significant segment of the black tradition will remain silent.

Oxford University Press, in collaboration with the Schomburg Center for Research in Black Culture, is publishing thirty volumes of these compelling works, each of which contains an introduction by an expert in the field. The set includes such rare texts as Johnson's *The Hazeley Family* and *Clarence and Corinne*, Plato's *Essays*, the most complete edition of Phillis Wheatley's poems and letters, Emma Dunham Kelley's pioneering novel *Megda*, several previously unpublished stories and a novel by Alice Dunbar-Nelson, and the first collected volumes of Pauline Hopkins's three serialized novels and Frances Harper's poetry. We also present four volumes of poetry by such women as Mary Eliza Tucker Lambert, Adah Menken, Josephine Heard, and Maggie Johnson. Numerous slave and spiritual narratives, a newly discovered novel—*Four Girls at Cottage City*—by Emma Dunham Kelley (-Hawkins), and the first American edition of *Wonderful Adventures of Mrs. Seacole in Many Lands* are also among the texts included.

In addition to resurrecting the works of black women authors, it is our hope that this set will facilitate the resurrection of the Afro-American woman's literary tradition itself by unearthing its nineteenth-century roots. In the works of Nella Larsen and Jessie Fauset, Zora Neale Hurston and Ann Petry, Lorraine Hansberry and Gwendolyn Brooks, Paule Marshall and Toni Cade Bambara, Audre Lorde and Rita Dove, Toni Morrison and Alice Walker, Gloria Naylor and Jamaica Kincaid, these roots have branched luxuriantly. The eighteenth- and nineteenth-century authors whose works are presented in this set founded and nurtured the black women's literary tradition, which must be revived, explicated, analyzed, and debated before we can understand more completely the formal shaping of this tradition within a tradition, a coded literary universe through which, regrettably, we are only just beginning to navigate our way. As Anna Cooper said nearly one hundred years ago, we have been blinded by the loss of sight in one eye and have therefore been unable to detect the full *shape* of the Afro-American literary tradition.

Literary works configure into a tradition not because of some mystical collective unconscious determined by the biology of race or gender, but because writers read other writers and *ground* their representations of experience in models of language provided largely by other writers to whom they feel akin. It is through this mode of literary revision, amply evident in the *texts* themselves—in formal echoes, recast metaphors, even in parody—that a "tradition" emerges and defines itself.

This is formal bonding, and it is only through formal bonding that we can know a literary tradition. The collective publication of these works by black women now, for the first time, makes it possible for scholars and critics, male and female, black and white, to *demonstrate* that black women writers read, and revised, other black women writers. To demonstrate this set of formal literary relations is to demonstrate that sexuality, race, and gender are both the condition and the basis of *tradition*—but tradition as found in discrete acts of language use.

A word is in order about the history of this set. For the past decade, I have taught a course, first at Yale and then at Cornell, entitled "Black Women and Their Fictions," a course that I inherited from Toni Morrison, who developed it in the mid-1970s for Yale's Program in Afro-American Studies. Although the course was inspired by the remarkable accomplishments of black women novelists since 1970, I gradually extended its beginning date to the late nineteenth century, studying Frances Harper's *Iola Leroy* and Anna Julia Cooper's *A Voice From the South*, both published in 1892. With the discovery of Harriet E. Wilson's seminal novel, *Our Nig* (1859), and Jean Yellin's authentication of Harriet Jacobs's brilliant slave narrative, *Incidents in the Life of a Slave Girl* (1861), a survey course spanning over a century and a quarter emerged.

But the discovery of *Our Nig*, as well as the interest in nineteenth-century black women's writing that this discovery generated, convinced me that even the most curious and diligent scholars knew very little of the extensive history of the creative writings of Afro-American women before 1900. Indeed, most scholars of Afro-American literature had never even read most of the books published by black women, simply because these books—of poetry, novels, short stories, essays, and autobiography—were mostly accessible only in rare book sections of university libraries. For reasons unclear to me even today, few of these marvelous renderings of the Afro-American woman's consciousness were reprinted in the late 1960s and early 1970s, when so many other texts of the Afro-American literary tradition were resurrected from the dark and silent graveyard of the out-of-print and were reissued in facsimile editions aimed at the hungry readership for canonical texts in the nascent field of black studies.

So, with the help of several superb research assistants—including David Curtis, Nicola Shilliam, Wendy Jones, Sam Otter, Janadas Devan, Suvir Kaul, Cynthia Bond, Elizabeth Alexander, and Adele Alexander—and with the expert advice of scholars such as William Robinson, William Andrews, Mary Helen Washington, Maryemma Graham, Jean Yellin, Houston A. Baker, Jr., Richard Yarborough, Hazel Carby, Joan R. Sherman, Frances Foster, and William French, dozens of bibliographies were used to compile a list of books written or narrated by black women mostly before 1910. Without the assistance provided through this shared experience of scholarship, the scholar's true legacy, this project could not have been conceived. As the list grew, I was struck by how very many of these titles that I, for example, had never even heard of, let alone read, such as Ann Plato's *Essays*, Louisa Picquet's slave narrative, or Amelia Johnson's two novels, *Clarence and Corinne* and *The Hazeley Family*. Through our research with the Black Periodical Fiction and Poetry Project (funded by NEH and the Ford Foundation), I also realized that several novels by black women, including three works of fiction by Pauline Hopkins, had been serialized in black periodicals, but had never been collected and published as books. Nor had the several books of poetry published by black women, such as the prolific Frances E. W. Harper, been collected and edited. When I discovered still another "lost" novel by an Afro-American woman (*Four Girls at Cottage City*, published in 1898 by Emma Dunham Kelley-Hawkins), I decided to attempt to edit a collection of reprints of these works and to publish them as a "library" of black women's writings, in part so that I could read them myself.

Convincing university and trade publishers to undertake this project proved to be a difficult task. Despite the commercial success of *Our Nig* and of the several reprint series of women's works (such as Virago, the Beacon Black Women Writers Series, and Rutgers' American Women Writers Series), several presses rejected the project as "too large," "too limited," or as "commercially unviable." Only two publishers recognized the viability and the import of the project and, of these, Oxford's commitment to publish the titles simultaneously as a set made the press's offer irresistible.

While attempting to locate original copies of these exceedingly rare books, I discovered that most of the texts were housed at the Schomburg Center for Research in Black Culture, a branch of The New York Public Library, under the direction of Howard Dodson. Dodson's infectious enthusiasm for the project and his generous collaboration, as well as that of his stellar staff (especially Diana Lachatanere, Sharon Howard, Ellis Haizip, Richard Newman, and Betty Gubert), led to a joint publishing initiative that produced this set as part of the Schomburg's major fund-raising campaign. Without Dodson's foresight and generosity of spirit, the set would not have materialized. Without William P. Sisler's masterful editorship at Oxford and his staff's careful attention to detail, the set would have remained just another grand idea that tends to languish in a scholar's file cabinet.

I would also like to thank Dr. Michael Winston and Dr. Thomas C. Battle, Vice-President of Academic Affairs and the Director of the Moorland-Spingarn Research Center (respectively) at Howard University, for their unending encouragement, support, and collaboration in this project, and Esme E. Bhan at Howard for her meticulous research and bibliographical skills. In addition, I would like to acknowledge the aid of the staff at the libraries of Duke University, Cornell University (especially Tom Weissinger and Donald Eddy), the Boston Public Library, the Western Reserve Historical Society, the Library of Congress, and Yale University. Linda Robbins, Marion Osmun, Sarah Flanagan, and Gerard Case, all members of the staff at Oxford, were extraordinarily effective at coordinating, editing, and producing the various segments of each text in the set. Candy Ruck, Nina de Tar, and Phillis Molock expertly typed reams of correspondence and manuscripts connected to the project.

I would also like to express my gratitude to my colleagues who edited and introduced the individual titles in the set. Without their attention to detail, their willingness to meet strict deadlines, and their sheer enthusiasm for this project, the set could not have been published. But finally and ultimately, I would hope that the publication of the set would help to generate even more scholarly interest in the black women authors whose work is presented here. Struggling against the seemingly insurmountable barriers of racism *and* sexism, while often raising families and fulfilling full-time professional obligations, these women managed nevertheless to record their thoughts and feelings and to *testify* to all who dare read them that the will to harness the power of collective endurance and survival is the will to write.

The Schomburg Library of Nineteenth-Century Black Women Writers is dedicated in memory of Pauline Augusta Coleman Gates, who died in the spring of 1987. It was she who inspired in me the love of learning and the love of literature. I have encountered in the books of this set no will more determined, no courage more noble, no mind more sublime, no self more celebratory of the achievements of all Afro-American women, and indeed of life itself, than her own.

A NOTE FROM
THE SCHOMBURG CENTER

Howard Dodson

The Schomburg Center for Research in Black Culture, The New York Public Library, is pleased to join with Dr. Henry Louis Gates and Oxford University Press in presenting The Schomburg Library of Nineteenth-Century Black Women Writers. This thirty-volume set includes the work of a generation of black women whose writing has only been available previously in rare book collections. The materials reprinted in twenty-four of the thirty volumes are drawn from the unique holdings of the Schomburg Center.

A research unit of The New York Public Library, the Schomburg Center has been in the forefront of those institutions dedicated to collecting, preserving, and providing access to the records of the black past. In the course of its two generations of acquisition and conservation activity, the Center has amassed collections totaling more than 5 million items. They include over 100,000 bound volumes, 85,000 reels and sets of microforms, 300 manuscript collections containing some 3.5 million items, 300,000 photographs and extensive holdings of prints, sound recordings, film and videotape, newspapers, artworks, artifacts, and other book and nonbook materials. Together they vividly document the history and cultural heritages of people of African descent worldwide.

Though established some sixty-two years ago, the Center's book collections date from the sixteenth century. Its oldest item, an Ethiopian Coptic Tunic, dates from the eighth or ninth century. Rare materials, however, are most available for the nineteenth-century African-American experience. It is from these holdings that the majority of the titles selected for inclusion in this set are drawn.

The nineteenth century was a formative period in African-American literary and cultural history. Prior to the Civil War, the majority of black Americans living in the United States were held in bondage. Law and practice forbade teaching them to read or write. Even after the war, many of the impediments to learning and literary productivity remained. Nevertheless, black men and women of the nineteenth century persevered in both areas. Moreover, more African-Americans than we yet realize turned their observations, feelings, social viewpoints, and creative impulses into published works. In time, this nineteenth-century printed record included poetry, short stories, histories, novels, autobiographies, social criticism, and theology, as well as economic and philosophical treatises. Unfortunately, much of this body of literature remained, until very recently, relatively inaccessible to twentieth-century scholars, teachers, creative artists, and others interested in black life. Prior to the late 1960s, most Americans (black as well as white) had never heard of these nineteenth-century authors, much less read their works.

The civil rights and black power movements created unprecedented interest in the thought, behavior, and achievements of black people. Publishers responded by revising traditional texts, introducing the American public to a new generation of African-American writers, publishing a variety of thematic anthologies, and reprinting a plethora of "classic texts" in African-American history, literature, and art. The reprints usually appeared as individual titles or in a series of bound volumes or microform formats.

The Schomburg Center, which has a long history of supporting publishing that deals with the history and culture of Africans in diaspora, became an active participant in many of the reprint revivals of the 1960s. Since hard copies of original printed works are the preferred formats for producing facsimile reproductions, publishers frequently turned to the Schomburg Center for copies of these original titles. In addition to providing such material, Schomburg Center staff members offered advice and consultation, wrote introductions, and occasionally entered into formal copublishing arrangements in some projects.

Most of the nineteenth-century titles reprinted during the 1960s, however, were by and about black men. A few black women were included in the longer series, but works by lesser known black women were generally overlooked. The Schomburg Library of Nineteenth-Century Black Women Writers is both a corrective to these previous omissions and an important contribution to Afro-American literary history in its own right. Through this collection of volumes, the thoughts, perspectives, and creative abilities of nineteenth-century African-American women, as captured in books and pamphlets published in large part before 1910, are again being made available to the general public. The Schomburg Center is pleased to be a part of this historic endeavor.

I would like to thank Professor Gates for initiating this project. Thanks are due both to him and Mr. William P. Sisler of Oxford University Press for giving the Schomburg Center an opportunity to play such a prominent role in the set. Thanks are also due to my colleagues at The New York Public Library and the Schomburg Center, especially Dr. Vartan Gregorian, Richard De Gennaro, Paul Fasana, Betsy

Pinover, Richard Newman, Diana Lachatanere, Glenderlyn Johnson, and Harold Anderson for their assistance and support. I can think of no better way of demonstrating than in this set the role the Schomburg Center plays in assuring that the black heritage will be available for future generations.

CONTENTS

INTRODUCTION

Joan R. Sherman

Mary Eliza (Perine) Tucker Lambert (1838–?) was the editor of *St. Matthew's Lyceum Journal* and author of *Life of Mark M. Pomeroy* (1868) as well as two volumes of poetry. *Loew's Bridge, A Broadway Idyl* (1867) is a poet's-eye view of lower Manhattan just after the Civil War; the poem's urban setting, its sixty-nine page length and footnotes, and its realistic vignettes of city life and contemporary events distinguish it from standard lyrics of the century.

The Loew's or Fulton Street Bridge spanned Fulton Street and Broadway for just a year in the mid-1860s. The poem's speaker views and records the stream of humanity passing under the bridge, and Lambert, in a note, states that "everything described was seen, if not precisely in the order mentioned." This all-inclusiveness and absence of an ordering principle give the poem a sprawling looseness; moreover, the observer's focus jumps and shifts among various times, places, and topics, breeding confusion and, at times, exasperation in the reader. For example, the speaker sees a "lawyer," ponders the law's lack of justice and mercy, and then compares the lawyer to the serpent in the Garden of Eden, which leads to reflections on "the world's a stage," to thoughts about plays and actresses, and then doctors and artists. In another section, a long "idyll" celebrating the marvelous invention of the sewing machine oddly interrupts the view from the bridge.

Lambert's description of the "passing throng" reveals her primary purpose as each character she describes generates a moral or social lesson. The fallen woman instructs us about guilt and women's frailty; Wall Street men chasing dollars and "apple women" with bank accounts teach that "Merit is nothing, money rules the day." Gems of sentimental patriotism arise from the scene of a Southern "warrior" giving alms to a one-armed ex-Union soldier playing "Dixie." The throng includes a child with his grandfather, a ragman, statesmen and city politicians, starving authors, peddlers, the poets William Cullen Bryant and Miles O'Reilly, and a host of other cityfolk whose appearances trigger homilies on Christian idealism, slavery, or the quality of New York's daily newspapers.

The poetry of *Loew's Bridge* is pedestrian, with trite rhymes and stock meters. Lambert is no Walt Whitman celebrating "Mannahatta" or ferrying across the East River. However, her panoramic vision provides a unique vehicle for wide-ranging thoughts and feelings, while here and there she lets us share her historical sense and participate in the crowded, colorful life of New York City.

In the same year as *Loew's Bridge*, Lambert published a 216-page volume of seventy-three conventional verses, none concerned with race. She handles varied metrical, rhyme, and stanza schemes skillfully as she versifies the traditional subjects of love and the sorrowful loss of love, youth, and friendship; death and reunion in heaven; the virtue of kindness and the vice of intemperance. In a few poems, Lambert finds a "close semblance, and fit moral" between nature—a hummingbird, mistletoe, flower buds—and human life; with rare humor in "Apple Dumplings," she cautions against equating the ungainly outside with the delicious inside of a pastry and a person.

Although a majority of verses in *Poems* are as "weary, weary, weary," as the item "Weariness," a few take up unusual subjects or employ a fresh, personal perspective. No other black poet of the century wrote a poem about a divorced father giving up his child ("Wail of the Divorced"); or an hysterical husband hallucinating ("Crazed"); or opium addicts, before and after their dose ("The Opium-eater"); or a double suicide ("Arria to Poetus"). The homeliness of "Upon Receipt of a Pound of Coffee in 1863" is welcome, as is the light irony of "The Beautiful Sea," which the poet loves until seasickness torments her. In her preface, Lambert concedes that her verses "may not be great, nor broad, nor deep" nor "beautiful," but she hopes they will "give to any soul the perfume of simple truthfulness and genuine feeling." We can grant these self-criticisms as well as appreciation for the originality of *Loew's Bridge*.

The name on her death certificate was "Menken Adele Isaac Barclay," and her tombstone read, "Adah Isaacs Menken." She was, perhaps, born Philomène Croi Théodore but assumed half a dozen pseudonyms over the years, identified five different men as her father, and claimed to have had six husbands in sixteen years. It is no wonder that since her death in 1868, "La Belle Menken" has been examined in ten full-length biographies (plus dozens of articles and parts of books); and even her latest and most reliable biographer admits, "I haven't found out who she was" (Wolf Mankowitz, *Mazeppa: The Lives, Loves and Legends of Adah Isaacs Menken* [New York: Stein and Day, 1982]).

Although her parentage (and birthdate) remain in doubt, much is known about Adah's brief tempestuous careers as the world's highest-paid actress, a celebrated writer and lecturer, the notorious mistress of famous men, and a poet. She probably was born in 1839 in New Orleans to Auguste Théodore,

a mulatto registered as a "free man of color," and his wife,
Magdaleine Jean Louis Janneaux. At the age of fifteen, in
Texas, Adah gave Shakespearean readings, published a few
poems, and married the first of her (authenticated) husbands,
Alexander Isaac Menken, a wealthy Jewish businessman. To
please Menken's family in Cincinnati, Adah invented Jewish
forbears for herself, studied Hebrew and the Bible, and wrote
highly acclaimed poems and articles on Jewish issues for the
Israelite. In her poem, "Hear, O Israel!," Adah portrays
herself as a militant "prophet" and leader of her adopted people: "But the God of all Israel set His seal of fire on my
breast, and lighted up, with inspiration, the soul that pants
for the Freedom of a nation!" Such identification with the
Jews' tragic history perhaps gave Adah the rootedness she
craved (as well as publicity for her stage career), and although she soon left Menken and Judaism, she did receive,
at her request, a Jewish funeral and burial.

The acting career of Adah, billed as "The World's Delight," began to immediate acclaim in New Orleans in 1856.
Beautiful, brash, ambitious, and sexy, Adah sang, danced,
and played comedic and romantic leads until she found, in
1862, the role that would give her immortality and riches:
In Byron's *Mazeppa*, the scantily clad Adah, chained to the
back of a horse, galloped across stages from San Francisco to
New York, London to Paris for six years until her untimely
death. Masterful publicity for her nearly nude performances,
her exuberant acting style, and the unrelenting press cover-
age of her scandalous private life packed theaters everywhere
and brought Adah the attentions of literary giants and royalty.

At Pfaffs in New York City, Adah dined with poets Fitz-
James O'Brien and Walt Whitman; in San Francisco, she

hobnobbed with Joaquin Miller, George Sterling, Artemus Ward, Bret Harte, and Mark Twain; in London, her poems impressed the Rossetti brothers, and she dedicated her only book of poetry, *Infelicia,* to Charles Dickens. Georges Sand, her close friend in Paris, was godmother to Adah's son, Louis Dudevant Victor Emmanuel Barkley (who died in infancy); and all the word gossiped over her outrageous love affairs with Alexander Dumas Père and Algernon Swinburne.

To her collection of famous friends and lovers, Adah added three more husbands: John C. Heenan, a prize-fighter (1859); Robert Henry Newell, better known as the satirist "Orpheus C. Kerr" (1862); and James Paul Barkley (1866). These marriages, which lasted a few days to a few months, brought Adah much grief and scurrilous attacks in the press. In spite of her enormous theatrical success, Adah felt she had failed at life because she was a woman without roots or identity save for the mythical personae she created, a woman who craved love but fell victim to men's manipulation and oppression, a woman scorned by a Victorian society for her free-living rebelliousness. Above all, Adah longed for appreciation as a woman of letters, a great poet; thus she struggled in the last year of her life to gather her poems from periodicals and friends, to design and publish the slim volume that contains about half her life's output. A week after Adah's death at age 29 (August 10, 1868), her *Infelicia* appeared to universally negative, often savage reviews of the poems and the poet.

The poet of *Infelicia* speaks with two voices: hysterical and extremely hysterical. In almost every poem, she "shrieks and groans" like the "ghosts of my dead hopes" in "Drifts That Bar My Door." This breast-beating lamentation, steeped in bitterness, disillusionment, self-denigration, and guilt for some unnameable sin, unhappily typifies Menken's verse. In the

same year as "Drifts," published in 1860 when she report-
edly was suicidal, came "Answer Me," a plea for security
and love so full of anguish and loneliness as to make a reader
gasp in pain. Enforcing her hopelessness, the poet employs,
as in "Drifts," dozens of rhetorical questions and a tolling
refrain. Elsewhere, through similarly dark glasses, Menken
sees her life as a wrecked ship, or herself a "victim" of "Cold
friends and causeless foes," ruined by love. "My vital air is
wretchedness," she accurately wails.

Two long, sprawling poems, each in six sections, cry of
lost love. "Resurgam" begins histrionically, "Yes, yes, dear
love! I am dead!/ Dead to you!/ Dead to the world!/ Dead
for ever!"; and "Sale of Souls" begins: "Oh, I am wild—
wild!" Both poems continue at a fever-pitch of despair, fear,
and passionate need, abruptly and incoherently shifting among
topics and directions. As the beginnings of these poems illus-
trate, Menken's favorite punctuation is the exclamation mark
(followed closely by the question mark): "Pitiless wind! Pitiless ocean!; "Waiting! Starving! Shivering!"; even the *titles*
of poems exclaim.

Some of her poetic techniques show the influence of three
poets she greatly admired, Poe, Swinburne, and Whitman.
Menken may have borrowed from Poe the brooding shadow
of death in her poems, images of terror-haunted graveyards,
demonic, ravenous waves that swallow ships, and the omni-
present spirit of melancholy. She may also be indebted to
Swinburne for her preoccupation with death and for the
grandiloquence of lines such as these from "Pro Patria.
America, 1861": "The soft Beam of Peace bronzed the rocks
of stern ages,/ And crept from the valley to burn on the
spire;/ And stooped from the glimmer of gems in the palace,/
To glow in the hovel a soul-heating fire."

Walt Whitman surely influenced Menken's verse. She wrote a courageous essay, "Swimming Against the Current," in praise of Whitman's *Leaves of Grass,* admiring the free-ranging boldness of his poetry, his idealism and historical sense, and his efforts "for the cause of liberty and humanity!" Far ahead of her contemporaries, Adah adapted Whitman's free verse for many of her poems; other Whitmanesque elements are the frank, defiant self-revelations of what she called her "wild soul-poems," the focus on "me, myself" of her impassioned first-person speakers, and the division of long poems into numbered sections. Her "Hear, O Israel!" suggests other Whitman influences: the Biblical source; repetition of the first words of lines; a sequence of imperative verbs: "Fear not . . . Rise up . . . Cast down . . . Look aloft . . . Come forth"; and incantatory rhythms. Although she lacked Whitman's breadth of subject, philosophical depth, and poetic control, her recognition of Whitman's greatness and her emulation of his style attests to her intelligence and artistic sensitivity. It is interesting, however, that Adah's most readable poems, "Aspiration" and "Infelix," express her feelings directly, unencumbered by imitation. "Aspiration" warns the "poor young Soul" that it must climb a treacherous path to the Olympus of poets. "Infelix" is her trademark, like "Infelicissima," "Infelicissimus," and "Infelicia," names she took to signify her unhappiness. Simpler in style than most of her poems and sincerely touching, "Infelix" chastises a faithless lover.

In contrast to the dull conventional poetry of her time, Adah's work is remarkably dramatic, intensely self-aware and "confessional," and unsparing in its condemnation of a male-dominated world that restricts woman's freedom, mocks her expressions of "genius," and dooms her, body and soul, to unhappiness. These qualities no doubt brought *Infelicia* the popularity among women that carried it through twelve editions from 1868 through 1902.

It seems fitting that Byron's *Mazeppa* brought renown to "the Menken," for she mirrored in her living and in the personae of her verse, who were identical to Adah, the combined natures of Lord Byron and his poetry's heroes. A complex and contradictory woman, Adah was an isolated wanderer, plagued by shifting moods of dark melancholy, passionate self-assertion, suicidal guilt, and childish delight; she was impetuous and gregarious yet self-absorbed, idolized by the crowd yet ostracized by them for her hostility to restrictive moral codes; she was extremely handsome and ardently pursued by lovers but unable to find a lasting love. Indeed a "Byronic" heroine, Adah knew the pain of *Childe Harold*, "The wandering outlaw of his own dark mind" (III:3), and she shared the fate of Lord Byron, a brave fighter for human rights and a romantic poet who died young.

Collected
Black Women's
Poetry

LOEW'S BRIDGE,

A

BROADWAY IDYL.

————▸●◂————

NEW YORK:

M. DOOLADY, PUBLISHER,

448 BROOME STREET.

1867.

JOHN J. REED, PRINTER AND STEREOTYPER,
43 Centre Street, New York.

A BROADWAY IDYL.

————◦—◦◦—————

FOR hours I stood upon THE BRIDGE, (¹)

Which looms like a volcanic ridge,

    Above a scathing fire below.

A flaming crater of burning hearts—

And, as souls passed beneath my feet,

As weary souls passed to and fro

A knowledge came, so sad, yet sweet,

    Each inner life I seemed to know.

Oh, heaven and earth! the sins and sorrows

That scarred each heart with countless furrows!

And yet I had a glimpse of love;

For maidens, pure as snow-white dove

     And innocent of guile,

All heedless of this world of pain,

     Passed under with a smile.

Bright rosy cheeks, the badge of health—

     Eyes dancing in their mirth—

And rose-bud lips as yet unpressed,

Soft golden hair, by none caressed,

     For save the passion born at birth,

And vanity the sin of wealth,

    Their hearts were pure, free of the lust,

    Which aye debases mortal dust.

And faces sweet as Poet's dream,

Sad as the fair Evangeline,

Or like Maud Muller, by the stream

    In the meadows raking hay,

Whose face betrays the " vague unrest "

Which drives from every human breast

    All happiness away.

Some seeking for their "Gabriel,"

Some mourning for lost " Judge."

Some hiding 'neath a smiling face

 The sorrow I know well,

The sorrow which makes hearts but graves,

 And faces monuments.

Full many a floweret passed beneath,

 Clasping the hand of sin,

And childish voices in merry glee,

 Made musical the din,

Like some sweet symphony which swells

 Amid the noise on battle field,

Waking, in many a heart, the wells

 Of some emotion

Long since dead to all save One
Who for us gave His only Son ;
    And over me a softness crept,
    And pining for my own, I wept.

Thank God for children ! for they give
New life to those who would not live,
But that the bonds, so holy bound,
Like some fresh vine, an oak around
Their aching hearts, too full of grief,
Which find in bondage sweet relief.
God bless each childish happy face,
Each fairy form so full of grace—

For without children life would be

　　　Devoid of all its purity.

An angel?　No, 'tis but a child of earth,

But Venus smiled at that fair maiden's birth.

True, Poverty has placed on her his mark

　　　Of scanty garments—

But tattered robes hide not the wealth and

　　　grace

That nature showered on hair, and form, and

　　　face.

Full many a childless parent would bestow

Gold, yellow glittering gold, could that fair child

With her pure face, by art's hand undefiled,

    Have been her very own.

But Nature sells not, freely does she give,

God in His wisdom, that we all may live

    Contented with our lot,

Gives mind and beauty to His favored few,

To some He grants more than their meed of

    wealth,

And to the rest He opes His store of health.

This child is leading by her gentle hand

    Her aged grandsire, on whose sightless eyes

The hand of Time has placed his seal of seals.

Nor will they open. until in the skies

Light of all light His glorious self reveals.

On, on they pass—but ah ! that piercing scream

Awakes me—is it but a dream ?

No ! there he stands in middle of Broadway

A frozen statue, moving neither way.

A horse is near him, and with instinct rare

The little child, who makes his life her care,

As if to shield him from approaching harm,

Twines her fair arms about his aged form.

I hold my breath; but ah, no need of fear,

The watchful guardian of the Bridge (²) is near,

Robed in his blue coat, with the star of gold,

Whose courage gives him mine of strength un-

      told ;

He hurls the horse back, and they onward move,

The loving guided by the hand of love.

A rag-man passes, clad in vesture poor.

    O scorn him not, for in his dirty bag

Is many a space for thoughts to rest upon—

    Of countless value is each little rag :

Like trifles they accumulate,

    And when they mingle into one,

By trying process changing state,

Upon their surface lurks the hate

    Or love, of many a nation.

'Tis well we think not, as we cast aside

The tiny fragments of our daily task,

Of the dread tidings those same rags may bring

    E'en to our door.

Some great man's fate, like Maximilian's doom,

May o'er even strangers cast a death-like gloom.

Some unjust act, a NATION put to shame,

Some lines of praise, but pages full of blame.

Praise give to poets, for 'tis poets' due,—

Worth should be granted to the rag-man too,

For in his hands the firm foundation lies,

Upon which poets' airy-castles rise.

Down, down from Romance's perch, my muse,

Wipe Fancy's dust from off thy shoes:

Let good and pure rest for a while,

Portray realities of guile.

Guile ?   Say, is there real guilt on earth ?

And shall we all be judged

By sins—not weakness ?

God forbid !

Mortals we are, conceived in sin—

None, none are pure, all " might have been,"

Had woman's heart been made of stone.

All, all are frail, and she who passes now

With stains of sin upon her pallid brow,

    And misery untold within her heart,

    I leave to Him who said,

" Neither do I condemn thee, go thy way

And sin no more," for what art thou but clay !

Weary and slow she passes 'neath the arch,

And now, upon her face I see a flush, as if her

        youth

Had been renewed by some glad truth,

As glancing up, into a manly face,

J. M. OTT N.Y.

She speaks her greeting with a pleading grace.

No word from him : naught save a smile of
scorn!

Alone she stands—he with the tide moves on.

All color from the flushing cheeks now dies,

Hands press her heart to stifle woe's deep cries.

And onward, moved by demon of despair,

She braves the " king of terrors " in his lair.

Say, is she saved ? Will the grim spectre,
Death,

Take from her more than life's short fleeting
breath ?

Doom her to endless misery of mind,

  Leaving a tainted name behind ?

Men swell the current,—many of them wear

Upon their brows the cruel badge of care.

The magic Greenback, like some rolling ball,

Gathers the man-moss, hurls them into "Wall." (3)

Each eager face in passing seems to say—

" Chasing a dollar, comrades, clear the way !

I am ambitious, and I fain would win :

Would gain the dollar even if I sin."

And oft, alas, in raging lust for gold,

Life's cup is broken, and a soul is sold !

Some push along with satisfaction's air,

While others wear the visage of despair.

Some, looking forward, in perspective see

When their one dollar shall ten thousand be.

Some glancing upward, building in the sky

Bright airy castles soon to fade and die :

While sad-faced men look backward and pass on

Cursing the day that ever they were born.

For empty pockets begets woes untold,

And friends and comfort vanish with our gold.

Then should we wonder that the trash is sought,

With which e'en friendship is oft sold and
      bought ?

There, mark the difference in the prosperous man,

And one who gains existence as he can—

One with his head erect, the other bowed,

The poor are humble, but the rich are proud.

Hark! surely there is music in the air!

    'Tis "Dixie" floating on this Northern breeze.

Thrilling each Southern heart with thoughts

    Of a lost Nation's hope, and her despair.

This world is strange, 'tis an anomaly!

For glancing downward now I see

A one-armed soldier, in a coat of blue—

And, by-the-by, his legs are missing too,

Grinding with his one hand the "Dixie" song.

Perchance, who knows, that very tune was
   played,

When in the midst of some mad martial raid
   The missile came along

Which left of noble manhood but the wreck.

Now, standing by his side, is one

I know, a warrior, brave for Southern rights:
   All strife is ended, and all warring done.

And the blue-clad soldier's eyes seem dancing
   lights,

   As in his hand the Southern warrior places

His mite ; true, 'tis a small donation,

But it betrays the great appreciation

    Of a brave soul, for spirit kindred born.([4])

Now " Yankee Doodle " falls upon my ear,

Then " Erin's Wearing of the Green " I hear ;

And as the human current moves along,

I read their Nation as each hears the song—

For faces speak, and eyes will tell the truth :

When Memory, with swift electric string,

Draws Past to Present, on sweet music's wing.

A tear in manhood's eye is no disgrace,

And pity lends a charm to every face.

Statesmen, the satellites of Fame,

    Are mingling with the throng,

Some heart sore with a Nation's blame,

    Some charmed by the Siren song

        Of present popularity.

Ah me! how changes tide with time,

    Public opinion is as vacillating

As seasons are, forever on the change.

Warm, temperate, cold, in changing only true,

Or like some serpent, with its roseate hue,

Of commendation, luring on its victim

E'en to death; who, wounded by the sting

Of misconception, like the poor snail,

Shrinks in his shell, and starving for fame,

    Dies in obscurity.

New eyes are mine—I see as ne'er before;

Not forms alone, as in the days of yore,

But acts—sins long untold—

And acts of mercy to my gaze unfold.

    I see too, lives of men,

And step by step, I trace some back to when

With ragged jacket, hatless head, and feet

Frozen and bare, they wandered in the street,

With hope, ambition, faith within their hearts,

    Whose dirty faces bore the stamp of MAN.

God's own insignia, neither wealth nor fame,

Nor right by birth to high ancestral name,

    Can grant such priceless boon.

The glory be to him who can declare

I am the founder of the name I bear.

Not the last scion of the great of earth,

But first ; the hour which gave me birth

Shall be remembered, until time shall be

    Lost in the mazes of Eternity.

One word of praise, and it is nobly won

For him who said, " I will win for my Son

    A name all glorious and bright."[5]

Censorious world! oh why not o'er the past

Oblivion's vail in its soft darkness cast

    And honor grant, for what one is not was.

Our City rulers pass in grand array,

Some whose each step pollutes this snowy way,

Whose nervous glances tell that they have sold

Their honor for position and for gold.

Others, whose pure lives can command

Respect, aye love, of all e'en in this land,

    Where merit's granted but to favored few.

Our present Mayor, with abstracted air,

Comes with kind greeting, for high, low and fair.

In each heart holds he a much envied place,

And his position fills with nameless grace.

And yet he bears upon his brow the badge

Of hope deferred, Ambition's goal half won—

The race for station only just begun.[6]

His rival follows, and determination

Within his eye shows will to do, or dare—

Not only will, but power,

Dame Nature's priceless dower.

From very foot the mount of fame he trod :

Sprung from the people, he's the people's god.[7]

And Authors, too, the devils of the quill,

Who daily, hourly their poor brains distil:

Exalted, trampled by the public will;

And yet they cater, and will cater still,

Undaunted by the missiles hurled

  Each day by a censorious world.

Some with their faces beaming bright

See in their eyes success' light;

Some who on yesterday were naught,

To-day they find themselves the sought

And courted, for their genius bright,

   A reputation

  Made by the " NATION,"

Growing like Jonah's gourd all in a night.

And some poor sinner who awoke

From dream of fame, alas to find

His fancy's child, child of his mind,

Damned by the critics,

      Or unnoticed passed.

Ah, well, when he is dead, perchance his name

May live forever, immortalized by fame.

Such is the world's great largess to the dead,

The genius who when living wanted bread.

'Tis marvellous how mortals can invent

The ways and means to increase worldly stores.

Scorn not beginnings, and each small thing prize,

From e'en a cord,(⁸) sometimes large fortunes

    rise.

Yon apple-woman, vender of small wares,

Stale lozenges, fruit, candy, and vile cakes,

Who sells to urchins pennies' worth of aches,

Has now the gold safe hoarded in the bank,

With which to buy high place in fashion's rank.

Merit is nothing, money rules the day

Right royally, with rare despotic sway.

Something familiar comes before me now,

A picture of the Southern cotton-plant.

Broadway to-day, with its white glittering shield,

Is not as pure as Southern cotton field;

    With flakes of snow bursting from bolls of

        green,

Like some imprisoned genius scorning to be

Confined by laws, which bind society,

And breaking bonds is wafted on the breeze

Of public favor, or gathered by the slaves

      Of Fashion, whose vile hands

        Pollute its purity.

True, fragments now and then

Are gently taken to the hearts of men—

White flowers of fancy oftimes sink to rest

Deep in the wells of some fair maiden's breast:

Pure in themselves, they yet become more fair

By contact with the holy thoughts in there.

Cotton and slaves, 'twas thus we counted gold,

The slaves are free, the free in bondage sold ;

And now some man with rare prolific brains,

Genius inventive, by the name of Gaines,

Has made a bitters of the cotton plant ;

Polluting thus the hitherto white name

By clothing it in the vile badge of shame.

White, glaring white, is all the earth below,

And Broadway seems a " universe of snow."

Or like the Ocean's silver-crested waves,

Upon whose breasts thousands of barks are

tossed ;

Some brave the storm,—by cautious pilots

mann'd,

Some strike on breakers, ere they reach the

land,

And are forever lost.

E'er yet the sun his quarter's course had run,

Buyers and sellers their day's work begun.

Behind the counter patiently they toil,

Nor mingle with the busy passing throng ;

Save here and there, an eager care-faced man,

Who wiping cold dew from his tortured brow,

Seeks "Wall," to borrow wherewithal to pay

The rude, insulting, taunting, clamorous crew,

Who all-importunate demand their due.

Teachers of truth, now with the throng pass by,

Some hypocrites, with sanctimonious air,

Sin in their hearts, upon their faces prayer.

Preaching the truth, and living but a lie,

Make me repeat this maxim ever good—

"I am more afraid of Error in the guise of

Truth,

Than Truth in garb of Error." (9)

Brave was the man, his heart was pure and
      strong,

Who, from the pulpit, said the world was wrong

To clothe the Prodigal in direst shame,

And bless the brother with a stainless name.

'Tis to the dying that the doctors give

The healing potion, that will make them live.

No, not the righteous did Christ come to save,

The weak need courage, not the strong and
      brave.

He passes now, upon his face a smile

That faces wear, when hearts are free from
      guile.

" Church of the strangers," ([10]) I have watched
      thy growth,

Have seen thee from a mustard seed spring
      forth,

And in thy towering majesty arise,

Until thy spreading branches touched the skies.

All honor be to him whose tender care

Has raised the sapling to a tree so fair.

And " Norwood's " author, whose great study's
      man

Seems seeking on this thoroughfare to find

Some subject for his mighty mind

    To dwell upon—

With which to charm the senses of the millions

Who throng to hear him, for he's Fashion's

    " rage,"

As one will be, who makes his church a theatre,

    His pulpit but a stage.

Religion in this wise, enlightened day,

  Is free to all, that is, if all have gold ;

The vilest sinner is absolved for pay,

    And to him wide the grand church-doors unfold.

But woe to him who fain would enter in

The gilded fold, whose poverty's his sin.

Now is the Hall clock on the stroke of One;

The Sultans of the journalistic art,

Some without brains, and many without heart,

Come forth to lord it, and in one short hour

The City 'll quake beneath its ruling power.

　　　The daily press,

　　Whose influence is almighty,

　　　Then it should

Feed greedy masses, with the pure and good,

Not gather like the great Jove-headed Wood,

The daily slander, or the last sensation,

Showing our shame to every foreign nation.

He's for the South! what care I if he is,

Good can be found here, we have evil South.

    The MAN I honor for his love of right

And justice, but my truthful muse

Can give no merit to the " Evening News."

The " Evening Mail " I grant an honored place

In the home circle, for its columns bear

Naught save the pure, no badge of our disgrace,

Nothing that Age or Youth would blush to see,

    or hear.

The Poet editor, (") whose graceful rhyme

Touches the heart like the soft, sweet chime

Of memory bells, approaches now.

His hair is silvered by the hand of Time,

But his eyes still beam with the youth sublime

That wells from the heart ; the poetic fire

That lives, and lives, through years and years,

Whose brightness is dimmed not by joys nor

tears.

Ah! now I see in the passing throng

A " prophet and poet," our " king of song,"(¹²)

The bard of Erin, as brave and true

A " Private," as ever wore the blue,

Whose bright lights of genius most brilliantly

     shine,

When kindled on altar of love and—wine.

Now comes a white-haired man with mild and

     lamb-like face,

Kind, gentle eyes, who bears an honored name,

     Beloved by friend, revered by even foe,

Wields the pen-sceptre with majestic grace, [13]

     Who, by example, soothed a people's hate,

And saved a nation from the cursing woe

And bitter shame of striking conquered foe—

Was once a farmer's lad in the old " Granite

    State."

The hardy sons of stern New England's soil,

Taught from their birth to fear not want, nor

    toil,

Bear not the marks of the most dire disease

That Southerners inherit,—love of ease

Well, times have changed, the galling cháin

    That made the black man bow

Subservient to a master's mighty will,

    Is broken for Eternity ;

And with that chain the cord that bound

Our Southern souls in idleness to earth,

Wealth earned by others, strown with lavish

        hand,

With but one power, the power to command,

      Is loosed,

And on Ambition's wings our eager soul

Can reach the mount, Ambition's much-prized

      goal,

And grasping to our hearts the spectre Fame,

We faint to find the goddess but a name.

Dreaming again! 'Ah, how the memory clings

To the dead past ; a touch but opes the door

Of the dim vista of departed years,

And phantoms of our hopes and fears,

In dreamy indistinct array,

Seem flitting up and down this snowy way.

A loaded wagon now, has ope'd the door—

" Wilcox and Gibbs' " machine—and nothing

more. ([14])

Now, I am in the sunny land of flowers,

And smell the perfume from the jasmine bowers;

By opened window sit I half my days,

Sewing the while, but stopping oft to gaze

At two bright fairies, who with sable friends

Hide, like the pixies,

Underneath the petals of some bright flower,

Whose clear celestial hue

My darlings shame, with their bright eyes of

blue.

They crown each other with the garlands fair,

The "grey-beard" mingles with their silken

hair

Like cords of silver, with the jet and gold,

Soft tiny hands are resting on my brow,

I too am crowned :

" I would have made your wreath of white,"

The eldest says, " you are so good,

But, mother, sister said that you were true,

And so we added all these violets blue."

My good machine partaking of my pride

Sang one sweet song, and made the stitches fine,

Making the children hers as well as mine.

'Tis half-past one, and now is seen

In countless numbers eager " limbs of law "

Wending their way to " Courtlandt " from "Nas-

　　　　sau,"

To while away an hour with " Smith and

　　　　Green." (15)

Their minds to fortify, with meat and drink,

Ex necessitate rei, to enable them to think.

Law! say, what is the law but power?

The strongest mind will rule the hour.

Right, justice, mercy, ah! where are they now?

Not in this land, or, if here, bound in chains,

And only loosed by the command of law,

To whose decree, howe'er unjust we bow,

In meek submission low.

This science intricate we trace

E'en to the dwelling place

Of our first parents;

Children of nature, and of God,

    They knew not there was sin

'Till Satan, in a lawyer's garb,

    Their Eden entered, and with him the light

    Or power of knowing wrong from right.

But, like his children of the present day,

By statements colored in a *legal* way,

And well instilled into his client's mind

By the rare subtleties of lore profound,

Sowing his seed into prolific ground,

He made the white black, and the darkness

       light,

Changed Adam's day into eternal night

By causing wrong appear to be the right :

    And ever thus, as serpents charm they, when

    They cast their glamour on the eyes of men,

    And their each word's a snare,—

    Of Lawyers then, ye innocent, beware !

This world's a stage, each mortal acts a part

Of life's deep tragedy.　A breaking heart

Is often hid beneath a smiling face.

Ye, over righteous, if this world's a stage,

Why scorn the mimic copy of life's page ?

Sermons are preached to touch the hearts of men:

No sermon ever moved my heart, as when

I heard sweet " Fanchon," on her bended

    knee, ([16])

Sending above to the kind Deity

      A maiden's holy prayer;

        And then and there

I too prayed that the ray divine

Within my sinful heart should shine.

Oft have I seen the eye of age grow dim

At the mere attitude of homeless " Rip." ([17])

No temperance lecturer could call the vow

Which once burst forth in passionate impulsive-

      ness,

From one who heard the play.

" Never, oh never, shall e'en the smallest sip,

So help me God, again pollute my lip

    Of aught that will intoxicate !"

Surely the spirits which surround us rise

And register such vows above the skies.

Now comes a spirit brave, I ween,

Who on the theater's board is queen,

But on this tragic stageof life,

When kinsmen were at war and strife,

    An angel ministering became. ([18])

In sable robes she stood by beds of death,

Wiped the death dews, and caught the latest
breath
Of the brave boys in blue,
Who are sleeping now in the silent grave,
That o'er all the land one flag might wave.
It waves—but its folds are dyed with the
blood
Of the murdered martyrs, the brave, the true,
Who wore the GREY, and who wore the BLUE !

" Physician, heal thyself !" I fain would cry
To those devoted to the healing art,
Who in vast numbers now are passing by :

Is there one wise enough to heal

  A wound in his own heart ?

Can healing potions which the Doctors give

Imbue the fainting with a wish to live ?

Can one relieve the sleepless nights of pain,

Ambition's meed, the torture of the brain

That ever grasps beyond, above, so high,

That all its efforts prove, alas ! in vain,

And weary, sinking to the earth,

It curses hour that gave it birth,

  Dies, or becomes insane ?

There comes an old, well known slouch hat,

Which hides no slouching soul beneath its

    shade,([19])

But one whose greatest power lies

In curing body by first healing mind.

Did they not know when the immortal Davis lay

    Within his prison cell,

That the Leach's skill was not in drugs,

Who healed and made him well?

They knew not, who the power of speech denied,

    Of histories in touch of hands;

    Of volumes in a glance.

How could they know? formed of earth's com-

    mon clay,

Of the magnetic cords which bind
The thoughts of those whose natures are refined,
Whose bodies are subservient to the mind.

Strange, how a mortal by the power of will
   And genius, tho' untutored can exalt
Himself, until he will appear
  A being from another sphere.
As unlike to the common throng
As rhyming jingle to a stately song.

Few days ago, I heard kind blessings showered
   Upon his head who now draws near: [20]

Who had opened the once closed portals

    Of a soul's doors.

A mother, with a fearful heart,

    Without one ray of hope,

Placed in this Doctor's hands her only child,

Whose beauty needed naught, save sight,

To make it seem an angel bright.

One stifled cry ! ' Oh, mother, is this light ?

'Twas   black   before,   and,   mother,   now 'tis

        white.

I see you, mother, and I see God too !'

The little child, with its pure instinct rare,

Felt that God's spirit surely must be there,

For mother taught Light was, at God's com-
        mand,

And God alone could hold light in His hand.

The seasons change, opinions change,

    And even senses change with time ;

In age we see not with the eyes

    We looked from in our youth's full prime.

Couleur de rose is turned to sober grey,

Which grows more sombre every hour and day ;

    And Fashion too, like all things here below,

Is ever changing, as the sunset cloud ;

First a vast mountain, then a fleecy shroud,

A mass of darkness, now of crimson hue,

Soft, silver-tinted, then a violet blue,

    Then blending all the shades in the rainbow.

Now Fashion's minions, in the last new style,

Pass and repass, disdaining the slight smile

    That curls the lip of ever scornful man,

Whose brains inventive all new styles design,

    From fancy gaiters to arranging hair.

I've studied Nature, and I've studied Art,

Can at a glance detect, in smallest part

Of a grand toilet, whose great Artist's skill,

Moulded the madam to her august will,

If from the fashion-plates of Harper's good

" Bazar," " Die Modenwelt " or " Magazine

Of Madam Demorest," the robes were made.

If the rival artists([21]) of the present day,

Which hold in Fashion's world the sway

     Of reigning queens,

Their wondrous genius used to create

The airy, fairy figures slight,

Which make this city full of light.

I know, if from our " Merchant Prince " was

     bought

The fabric rare, made in a foreign land,

Upon whose very surface seems inwrought

A sightless eye, a wasted, helpless hand

Of some poor wretch, who e'en his senses gave

To deck the garment over which we rave.

Those tasty habits, costly, plain, and neat,

Disclosing 'neath their folds two tiny feet,

Snugly encased in leather-shoes thick soled,

Are snares which catch the unwary heart of

     man ;

Those costly jewels, too, from "Browne and

     Spaulding's" bought—

Are many a lesson to the wedded taught,

That Fanchon bonnet, ribbon and a flower,

Speak to man's pocket with all potent power.

But Fashion, although charming for a while,

Has not the lasting power of a smile.

Broadway! all glorious and grand, the city's
       heart;

A panorama! on the changing scene I gaze
    With reverential awe.

Work of man's hand—proof of a mortal's skill,

Who moulds such structures to his mighty will.

Once, where the "Herald" palace stands,

The red man claimed his home and lands.

One hundred years ago Hans smoked at ease

On summer eve, beneath the sheltering trees

Which grew where now the " Leader," " Tri-

bune," " World,"

Is daily, weekly, to our gaze unfurled,

Sending abroad the city's different views

Of national affairs.

Where stands the office of the Surrogate and

" Times,"

A church-bell pealed its sweet and solemn

chimes,

Not twenty years ago.

So the huge building rears its stately head

Above the city of the sainted dead.

Thrice haunted spot! for when the Hall clock

Strikes the hour of ten each night,

One gifted with a two-fold sight

Can witness scenes, scenes so appalling, drear,

That common souls would faint to even hear.—

First comes the red man, brandishing in air

His tomahawk, showing despair

 Upon his dusky face;

Then, with triumphant stare,

He waves above his head the hair,

Dripping with gore, of newly murdered foe.

His pale wife follows, and a sad surprise

Rests on her face, and in her mournful eyes.

They seem to miss the grand old forest trees,

And with the wail, " No home ! no place of

rest !"

They vanish as they came.

Fantastic forms in dress of olden times

Enter at will, through each self-opening door,

Or oft arise in seeming through the floor,

Chanting with solemn voices, old sweet hymns;

Such good old tunes, as in the days of yore

Made echoes ring from hill-side, and from shore.

Old wrinkled dames,—men in their manhood's

prime,

And round-faced maidens, with their locks of
           night,

Their crimson cheeks, and eyes so full of light,

Linger a moment, and then fade away.

Men robed in later styles the dark halls fill,

Hold eager consultation ; then a thrill

Of indignation seems to move the mass,

And to the office of the Surrogate (²²) they
           throng,

In a chill current, like the whirlwind strong—

And eagerly they seek, in each small nook to
           find

Some traces of the WILL they left behind.

Some smiling faces look upon me now,

But many glance, with a dark lowering brow,

Upon the fragments of a broken will.

In deep sepulchral tones, amid the ghostly din,

A stern voice utters, " Bring the culprit in."

    And the last Surrogate

Is ushered in, and takes his chair of state ;

Grim Death is standing by his head,

And o'er him spirits of the happy dead

    Are keeping watch.

Orphans and widows, with all patience wait

To hear the verdict of the Surrogate.

He tears the *will*, declares 'tis LAW's command,

And in a moment all the ghostly band

Have vanished, save the solemn clerk

Who writes until earth's pall of night

Is changed for robes of glorious light.

Shadows on the snow are lying,

Day is dead, the year is dying;

Wailing winds around are sighing

For the year that now is dying.

Tell me, year, before thy fleeting,

Tell me what will be the greeting

Of the year we'll soon be meeting,

Are the hopes that fill me, cheating?

Old year, whisper—still I listen!

Are hopes only drops that glisten

For a moment, as they christen

    Rose-buds newly born?

And the old year tells me, dying,

In the voice of winds soft sighing—

" Child of earth, cease, cease thy crying,

    What is life but hope?

Old year, give me e'er thy leaving

Token, that I may cease grieving ;

Make my faith pure, keep me believing

    Both in man and God.

Silver clouds are o'er me sailing,

And the strickened year fast paling,

Softly whispers 'mid the wailing—

    " I leave thee Love and Hope."

NOTES.

As this Book is expected to have considerable circulation outside the limits of the City, it has been suggested that a few Notes be appended, explanatory of the localisms contained therein :—

NOTE 1.

Loew's, or as it is commonly called, Fulton Street Bridge, was completed March, 1866, the building being supervised by the Hon. Charles E. Loew, whose name has been bestowed upon it by an Act of the Common Council of New York.

It is a large aerial structure, at the intersection of Broad-

way and Fulton Street, where the thoroughfare is continually
thronged with vehicles of all kinds, rendering it almost im-
possible for pedestrians to pass.

NOTE 2.

Only for readers not familiar with New York would it be
necessary to say, that this refers to the Police.

NOTE 3.

Wall Street is our temple of Mammon, where men of
money "most do congregate."

NOTE 4.

This is no fancy sketch. The writer actually saw this,—
saw a Southern soldier give alms to the Northern soldier,
who can be seen at any time near the Bridge playing an

organ. Indeed everything described was seen, if not precisely in the order mentioned.

NOTE 5

It is but common justice to say that this manly sentiment is reported of the Hon. John Morrissey.

NOTE 6.

Hon. John T. Hoffman is Mayor of New York at this writing, November 11th, 1867.

NOTE 7.

And the Hon. Fernando Wood, the rival candidate for the Mayoralty.

NOTE 8.

Always at the Bridge are venders selling the dancing toys, whose motions depend upon an elastic string, the invention of which has brought a fortune to the inventor.

NOTE 9.

This quotation is from Rev. Dr. Deems, and the allusion to "the prodigal," refers to a sermon preached by Dr. Deems, in which he represents the elder brother as worse than the prodigal. A report of that discourse, which produced a great impression on its delivery, appears in "Every Month," for September, published by S. T. Taylor.

NOTE 10.

"The Church of the Strangers," the name of a congregation composed of persons of all denominations, mostly strangers in New York; and its pastor, Dr. Deems, is abundant in labors among the sick, the poor, and the prisoner, and those who have no friends. It gives the author pleasure to say a word for an enterprise so catholic and so beneficial.

NOTE 11.

Perhaps it is superfluous to mention the name of the venerable William C. Bryant, of the "Evening Post."

NOTE 12.

"Miles O'Reilly" is the well known name of Gen. Charles G. Halpine, who is justly called our "King of Song," and who has written certain beautiful things, which will be remembered long after his career as a politician shall have been forgotten.

NOTE 13.

With whatever power Hon. Horace Greeley does anything, the wielding of the pen. is the only thing he is accused of doing "with grace."

NOTE 14.

The "Wilcox and Gibbs' sewing machine," celebrated

alike for its simplicity, rapidity of movement, as well as its durability, was patented in 1857, first sold in 1859, since which time one hundred thousand have been sold.

NOTE 15.

A well known and excellent restaurant in Cortlandt street.

NOTE 16.

Maggie Mitchell, the fascinating actress, has made this character memorable.

NOTE 17.

Play-goers will always know Joe Jefferson by his remarkable impersonation of "Rip Van Winkle."

NOTE 18.

Mrs. Gen. Lander, our American actress, is believed to surpass Ristori in the character of Elizabeth. Her goodness is equal to her greatness, as her attentions to the soldiers during the war demonstrates.

NOTE 19.

Dr. J. J. Craven, the physician attendant on Jefferson Davis at Fortress Monroe, and author of "Prison Life of Davis."

NOTE 20.

This actually occurred in the practice of Edward B. Foote, **M.D.**, the celebrated medical and electrical therapeutist, and author of "Medical Common Sense."

NOTE 21.

The artists referred to, are Madams **M. F.** Gillespie and Demorest, whose exquisite taste has rendered them renowned in the fashionable circles, not only of New York, but of the whole United States.

NOTE 22.

Hon. Gideon J. Tucker, who has held important State offices for more than twenty years, and is one of the first political writers of the age, is the present Surrogate of New York, and has occupied that position for the last five years. It is said of him that he has never been politically wrong in his life.

POEMS.

BY

MARY E. TUCKER.

Mary E. Tucker

POEMS.

BY

MARY E. TUCKER.

NEW YORK:

M. DOOLADY, PUBLISHER,

448 BROOME STREET.

1867.

JOHN J. REED, PRINTER AND STEREOTYPER,

43 Centre Street, N. Y.

TO

HONORABLE CHARLES J. JENKINS,

Governor of Georgia,

AND TO

MRS. GOVERNOR JENKINS,

MY HONORED AND TRUSTED FRIENDS,

My First Volume

IS

RESPECTFULLY AND AFFECTIONATELY

DEDICATED.

PREFACE.

————•••————

Out of a simple woman's heart these
rivulets of rhyme have run. They may
not be great, nor broad, nor deep. She
trusts that they are pure. She wrote these
verses often in sorrow, perplexity and distress. She publishes them in the hope that
they may be *souvenirs* of the years and the
scenes which cannot die out of the memory
of this generation. She lays this simple
offering on the altar of our common
country's literature. She will feel rewarded
if though these buds and flowers be not

very beautiful, they give to any soul the perfume of simple truthfulness and genuine feeling. "Homely" was once an endearing epithet, reminding the heart of its most sacred earthly associations. In this sense, the writer will be gratified to have her poems pronounced "homely."

CONTENTS.

———•◦•———

THE FIRST GREY HAIR.

NO, let it stay.   It speaks but truth :
      My Autumn's day is dawning.
The dream is past ; sweet dream of youth.
      Hair, I accept thy warning.
With mournful thought, my spirit swells,
At the wild chime of memory bells.

Why will we in the present time,
      Of by-gone days be dreaming ?
Say, why throughout the storm sublime,
      Is lightning ever gleaming ?
Ah ! there is naught on earth that quells
The chiming of sad memory bells.

Hope, garlands fair of future bliss,
    With Fancy's pearls is weaving ;
Alas ! we find in world like this,
    That Hope too is deceiving,
As on the past, our full heart dwells,
At your sad chiming, memory bells.

In youth all Earth was passing bright,
    And life with joy was teeming—
But hidden in each flower was blight,
    And happiness was seeming.
Yet charm me with your mystic spells—
With your sweet chiming, memory bells.

Why speak ye of the cruel wrong,
    That I am ever grieving ?
I would forget, forgive, be strong,
    With faith in Christ, believing.
But oh ! the strain triumphant knells—
Cease, cease your clashing, memory bells.

Avaunt, dark image of despair !
    Why dost thou still go raving ?
I would to Lethe's streams repair,
    And drown thy taunts in laving.
Alas ! can nothing still thy yells ?
Cease, cease your clashing, memory bells.

Now mournful is the solemn strain,
    And sadly I am weeping.
For those I love in battle slain,
    Who all unknown are sleeping,
Like murmuring of ocean shells,
Swells your sad requiem, memory bells.

Now much loved voices in their glee
    Their joyous shouts are sending ;
And the sweet chorus, light and free,
    Of many a song is blending,
Yet bitter tear-drops, sad fare-wells,
Melt in your chiming, memory bells.

Yet I would fain recall the past,
  The bright celestial gleaming,
Which my first love around me cast,
  Too sweet to be but dreaming.
Like flowing water, in lone dells,
Is your sweet chiming, memory bells.

Yes, silver hair, rest thee in peace,
  I know that life is waning,
That soon will all my troubles cease,
  And I, the goal attaining,
Will list the joy your music tells,
And love your chiming, memory bells.

FOUND—WHO LOST?

LADY, tell me, will you, pray,
     Why that cheek of roseate hue ;
Why so downcast, fond, yet shy,
     Is thine eye of heavenly blue ?

Let my eye gaze into thine ;
     Let me scan each fold of hair ;
Let me gaze upon thy cheek—
     By George ! I've found the secret there.

Lady, lady, tell me, pray,
     How you could do a thing so rash ?
Found what was not lost by you,
     One little hair from dark moustache !

So firmly printed on thy face !
  There—I detach it from the spot ;
Now blush no more—thy secret's safe.
  Known but to me, I'll tell it not.

"DID YOU CALL ME, FATHER?"

She opened the door, and said in an alarmed tone : "Father, was that you calling me?" And again, "Father!" And once again, after listening, "Father! I thought I heard you call me twice before!" No response.

Dickens' "Mutual Friend."

"DID you call me, Father?" Ah no,
      'twas the surge,
  Swelling a requiem, wailing a dirge :
  Back, maiden ! create still thy images rare,
  Thy bright glowing castles, so frail yet so fair.

"Did you call me, Father?" He hears thee no
      more,
  Life's tide has run out, he has drifted ashore ;
  No bright angels guided the sinner's frail bark—
  He was wrecked on the breakers, alone, in
      the dark.

" I thought that I heard you call twice before this,
　　And, Father, I felt on my brow your last kiss ;
　　Come back to me, Father, come back to your child,
　　Ere you be in the darkness, by false lights
　　　　beguiled."

Go gaze in the hollow, way down by the flare,
　　Say, beautiful dreamer, what seest thou there ?
　　Not the form of thy Father, cold, silent, and dead,
　　With the waves, and winds toying around his
　　　　grey head.

Thou seest the future, bright, happy and free,
　　When thy present through veil of past years
　　　　thou shalt see :
　　Now, garlands of hope, with thy love, and faith
　　　　blend,
　　All fading, alas ! as the gold sparks ascend.

Did you call me, Father ?   No, 'twas but the
      wind,
As searching, and prying, some secret to find ;
It wailed round the dwelling, again sought the
      shore,
And lifted the rags from the body once more.

His grey hair is all stiff, with the cold ocean brine,
His eyes have a look which no word can define—
As if in his struggles, while borne by the tide,
He thought of his darling, he called her, and died.

" Did you call me, Father ?"   Awake, girl, awake !
Thy burden of sorrow, within thy heart take ,
Awake from thy dreaming, each joy's fraught
      with care,
And Life's but a " hollow, way down by the flare."

THE BLIGHT OF LOVE.

MANY long years ago, I loved a youth,
    Who seemed the soul of honor and
       of truth—
He charmed my heart with some unholy spell,
He was a serpent, whom I loved so well.

The blush of girlhood had just ting'd my cheek ;
He knew me young—perchance he thought me weak.
'Tis said, he often boasted of his power,
To gather for his own each new-blown flower.

My simple language can not well describe
How first he stood before me in his pride ;
His form was cast in beauty's manly mould ;
His eyes shot fire, and his hair was gold.

Fain, fain would I describe to you his glance ;
One look enough, to throw me in a trance ;
His flute-like voice—ah ! from my sleep I woke,
When on mine ear the cadence gently broke.

A month passed by : he lingered by my side,
Longed for the time, when I should be his bride ;
Ah ! bitter ending, of that month of years,
A life of sorrow, and a life of tears.

The scathing truth, like any lightning stroke,
Fell'd me to earth, and my poor heart was broke ;
He, frightened, turned and left me, with my woe,
For, in my wrath, I sternly bade him go.

I've never loved again ; for there, and then,
All my faith vanished in the truth of men.
Of that short month, 'tis seldom that I speak,
And to forget my youth, in vain I seek.

HEART'S EASE.

LONELY and dreary was the day,
     Lonely and weary swelled my heart,
Fainting for need of Hope's bright ray—
     For without Hope will Joy depart.

We may survive, but do we live
     As God has willed his children should,
While craving, praying, give, oh give,
     All, all is evil, give me good ?

I wandered far from haunts of men—
     Cold, bitter cold, the North wind blew ;
It even reached my favorite glen,
     Where first spring flowerets always grew

I threw myself in my despair
    Upon a bed of faded leaves—
I wept aloud, and tore my hair,
    Grieved, as a bereaved mother grieves.

I prayed for death ; for death will bring
    Oblivion, and rest, sweet rest !
Then memory will lose its sting,
    And peace is found on Jesus' breast.

Give me, oh Father, was my prayer,
    Some token, that my Spring is near,
Soothe my deep grief, calm my despair,
    Console me, Lord, assuage my fear.

A sunbeam cleft the dense, cold air,
    And rested on a Heart's Ease bloom ;
Life, life in death ! adieu, despair !
    The morning dawns o'er night's deep gloom.

I clasped the omen to my soul,
    And to my lips the Heart's Ease pressed,
Tumultuous storms may o'er me roll—
    That token future joys expressed.

MY MOTHER'S VOICE.

OH never on my youthful ear
  A Mother's gentle accents broke !
The vital spark, from which I sprung,
  Expired, as I to life awoke.

No mother pressed me to her breast,
  And bade my childish heart rejoice,
For with my infant first-born wail,
  Death hushed for aye my mother's voice.

Alone I climbed the dizzy height,
  That led to never-dying fame,
I sought and won, and now I wear
  A famous, but unenvied name.

Had she been near, to shield and guide
    Her wayward, but her trustful child,
Rare flowerets would have bloomed where now
    Are weeds in rank luxuriance, wild.

In visions, sometimes, I behold
    Her form of heavenly loveliness ;
She speaks, and o'er me gently bends,
    And prints on my pale brow a kiss.

And I awake—'tis but a dream !
    But still the voice strikes on mine ear,
And from my callous heart calls forth
    Up through mine eyes the scorching tear.

Then pass not judgment rash, or harsh,
    On stern Misfortune's chosen child,
Who never heard a mother's voice,
    On whom a mother never smiled !

ADIEU.

LIFE is full of mirth and pleasure,
    But all joy is on the wing—
Base alloy corrodes each treasure,
    And enjoyment hides a sting.
Bliss is like a rainbow, cheating,
Beautiful and bright, but fleeting.

True, there's real bliss in the greeting
    Of each loving, kindred heart ;
But a sadness dims our meeting,
    For we know we soon must part—
Thus ties of Love, and friendship true,
Are severed by the sad adieu.

Adieu, and from the mother's eyes
    Streams her deep love, in tears.
Adieu, adieu, my child, she cries,
    Adieu, perchance for years.
And of our parting, keep this token,
My bitter tears—my heart is broken.

And that mother, in her anguish,
    Prays to God that she may die—
Better thus, than still to languish,
    Crying ever, this sad cry :
Give me back my child, my treasure,
Ye have o'erflown my bitter measure.

Alas ! the hand of reckless fate,
    As on time's wings, she flies ;
Severs, with most remorseless hate,
    The tenderest, holiest ties.
E'en sacred bonds of heaven's making,
Fate laughs to scorn, and smiles in breaking.

Thus all earthly friendships sever—
 Such is Heaven's stern decree.
But God's loved ones meet, to never
 Part again in land of free,—
There, there above the sky's deep blue,
Hearts are not broken by adieu.

I SMILE, BUT OH ! MY HEART IS BREAKING.

I MINGLE with the young and gay,
   In halls where Fashion holds her sway;
I gaze upon the giddy throng,
While for some quiet spot I long.

They call me heartless.   Do they know
That mirth is but an empty show ?
That silvery grandeur often shrouds
The storms which lurk within bright clouds ?

The eye may beam with dazzling light,
And shed on all its glances bright,
Yet be unburdened of the tears,
That shone like diamonds there, for years.

The lips may breathe the thoughtless word,
And yet, too oft alas ! unheard,
That word may mingle with a sigh
From reckless heart which prays to die.

I seek each joy—I fain would lave
My restless mind in Lethe's wave ;
But memory is ever waking—
I smile, but oh, my heart is breaking.

THE CRUSHED FLOWER.

A S through earth's garden once I strayed
        I saw a rose tree fair—
And from it plucked an opening bud,
        In all its beauty rare.

I gazed deep in its heart of hearts—
        It blushed beneath my eye ;
While its faint fragrance seemed to breath
        A gentle, unheard sigh.

'Twas mine alone !   I cherished it—
        My frail and lovely flower !
Until another bud I found,
        More beauteous, in an hour.

Then with relentless hand I broke
    The floweret's fragile stem :
I spoiled the gem that would have graced
    A monarch's diadem !

But stern remorse soon touched my heart,—
    Back to the spot I rushed.
Alas ! too late ; my flower was there,
    But its poor heart was crushed !

THE OLD CRIB.

"Sell that crib? Indeed! indeed 1 cannot, for I see in it the faces of my children. I will starve before I sell that crib."

Confederate Lady, 1864.

I KNOW thou art a senseless thing,
 Still recollections round thee cling
  Of joys long past ;
And I would fain retain thee now,
Yet want's stern hand and lowering brow
  Has o'er me cast
His misery with weight untold,
And, much prized crib, thou must be sold !

Ah ! well do I remember yet,
Remember ? can I well forget
  That happy day,

When a swift tide my spirit moved,
And with a mother's soul, I loved
    The child that lay
Within thy lap—my precious boy !
How throbbed my heart with untold joy.

How swiftly, then, the years sweep on,
With love, joy. wealth, they come, are gone,
    And very soon
A little dark-eyed, bonny girl,
Pressed on thy pillow many a curl.
    Most precious boon
That ever was to mortal given—
A cherub, from the gates of heaven.

And yet again, some powerful spell,
Called to this earth, sweet baby Bell,
    My sunbeam child,
With hair of gold, and eyes of blue,
And cheeks that vie the rosebud's hue—
    Pure, undefiled !

About my heart she seems to twine,
As round the oak, the clinging vine.

Take back thy gold !　It shall not go !
'Twas mine in weal, and now in woe :
　　It comforts me.
It takes me back, in fitful gleams,
To the sweet, fairy land of dreams,
　　And then I see
Those little heads, with glossy curls,
My manly boy, my little girls !

CHRISTMAS EVE, SOUTH, 1865.

POVERTY, remorseless spectre,
  Reigns throughout our once fair land,
And he wields no fancy sceptre,
  In his iron-covered hand.
Stifled sighs our hearts are rending,
Thanks for peace—with want contending.

Widows, orphans, homeless, dreary,
  Call in vain for earthly aid,—
There is rest for all the weary,
  On Him, let your cares be stayed.
He his helpless ones protecting,
Who abideth his directing.

'Tis the merry Christmas even,
  Hallowed throughout all the earth ;
Angels, too, rejoice in Heaven,
  O'er the blessed Saviour's birth.
Yet many are sad vigils keeping
For those who all unknown are sleeping.

Children hush their eager voices,
  They by instinct seem to feel,
That the heart which now rejoices
  Must, indeed, be cased in steel.
Yet still they turn with bitter sighing,
To where their little socks are lying.

" Mother ! mother ! darling mother !
  Please don't weep so any more ;
We are left you, I and brother,
  We don't care if we are poor.
Now, mother, darling, stop your weeping,
And kiss us ere we both are sleeping."

Rosy sleep at last has bound them ;
　　Now they revel in their dreams ;
" Santa Claus" now hovers round them,
　　Showering o'er them fairy gleams
Darlings, what is life but dreaming ?
Grasp a pleasure—'tis but seeming.

Mother ! kneel in adoration,
　　That thou hast some comfort left ;
Send forth, now, thy invocation
　　For the sad of all bereft.
With faith in God, in Christ believing,
For Heaven is real, and earth deceiving.

ARRIA TO POETUS.

IN vain ! in vain ! my pleading all in vain !
    Have I my senses, or am I insane !
Is it a dream, a fearful, bloody dream,
In which a mirage something real doth seem ?

Or is it truth, truth, stunning real, yet truth,
That pales with age the sunny hair of youth ?
Truth, nearest truth, that lying earth can give,
That thou hast, Poetus, but a day to live.

Have they no pity, or have they no shame,
That they should blacken thy illustrious name ?
It is not death.   Then dost not fear to die,
For thy pure soul will waft to God on high.

'Tis the disgrace, the ignominious end,
That our captors on thee fain would send.
Ah ! we will thwart them, Poetus : you and I
Will show how well the noble brave can die.

And God will pardon.   He, the God of love,
Will let us rest together, far above.
Ah, earth is fair and beautiful to see ;
But what are joys, my husband, without thee ?

To me, this dungeon is a palace gay,
For thou, beloved, art my soul's bright ray ;
But wert thou gone, each day would seem to me
Years, years, on years, a dark eternity.

Ah ! death is nothing but a moment's pain,
'Tis but the breaking of a link of chain,
'Tis but the ebbing of the tide of life,
'Tis but the leaving of this world of strife.

'Tis but the fading of a summer's flower,
To bloom again in Heaven's blissful bower ;
'Tis but the ending of a verse of time,
To add to death but yet another rhyme.

'Tis but the changing of the robes of earth
For spotless garments of immortal birth ;
Then, husband ! lover ! let us welcome death,
Our foes defy with e'en our latest breath.

This dagger, see how sharp its shining blade !
But one slight blow, and then death dues are paid.
She placed the knife upon her faithful breast—
Forgave the conquerors, and her husband blest.

Then plunged it in, and faintly, sweetly cried,
It is not painful, Poetus, and she died.
The faithful husband grasped the glittering knife,
And with his hand the forfeit paid of life.

TO MARY.

THE sky low down in distant West, is tinged
    with golden hue,
While all the glorious vault above is one brignt
    mass of blue.
Now as I still gaze in the West, my favorite
    star I see,
A diamond bright, queen of the night, the
    evening star for me.

Some love the warlike star of Mars : he pleaseth
    not my eyes ;
Some say that Jupiter is bright : his looks I
    little prize ;
The morning star is passing fair, but still I love
    it not ;
For none to me shines lovingly, as Venus* on my cot.

* Written when Venus was evening star.

Now the pale moon, as if in love, is sending from
      the sky
Her tender beams upon the field, where, Mary,
      you and I
So oft have stood at close of day, and talked our
      little cares—
Love, children, cooks, our thoughts of books, our
      prospects, hopes and fears.

Now standing out in bold relief, I see your cottage
      white ;
The once green trees are bare of leaves, they fell
      at winter's blight.
All is so still ! No light is there, I know you
      are at rest ;
May slumber's light be yours this night—may you
      be ever blest.

Soon, very soon, for aught we know, our pathway
      may divide ;
But, Mary, will you think of me, when I'm not by
      your side ?

And oh ! look on, with pitying eye, in distant,
      distant years ;
My virtues few, my friendship true, and o'er my
      faults shed tears.

SPRING.

SPRING, glad Spring, has dawned on earth ;
    Birds rejoice for her bright birth ;
  Farewell now to winter dear—
  Spring, with all her joys, is here.

  Trees clothed in green, our hearts' delight,
  Rare flowerets bloom, in colors bright ;
  Earth joyful now, her riches yields,
  While Spring her radiant sceptre wields.

  Lowing kine with thanks rejoice ;
  Insects hum with drowsy voice ;
  Everything on earth, in air,
  Join in the chorus, Spring is fair !

But now, alas, no transient bloom
Can take from each sad heart its gloom ;
For misery, with might untold,
Rests on each heart of mortal mould.

We mourn, because war's chilling blast
Its arm of death has round us cast ;
We mourn the noble and the brave,
Now sleeping in an unknown grave.

REVENGE.

A H ! I could curse them in my woe,
 E'en as the viper stings,
And to the heel that strikes it clings,
So I could plant my blow.

Yes, I could pray that fell disease
Should torture them with pain—
That plague should fall in every rain,
Miasma taint each breeze.

That wealth should vanish, and the curse
Of poverty should reign ;
That cries for bread should be in vain !
An always empty purse.

That friends should die, and every pride
Should vanish in a day ;
'Till even hope withdraws her ray,
And naught of joys abide.

Yes, I could whisper in the ear
Of one who loves to tell
Some fabrication, dark as hell,
As scandal loves to hear.

Revenge is sweet ; I could invent
Full many a thousand way,
That would my heartfelt wrongs repay,
Could they my soul content.

But could I go to sleep in peace,
And could I dream of heaven—
Could I e'er hope to be forgiven
When death came to release ?

Revenge is sweet to those who live;
But when we think of death—
The ebbing of this life-tide breath—
'Tis sweeter to forgive.

LIFT ME HIGHER.

LIFT me higher !   Lift me higher !
　　From this sphere of earthly dross ;
Upward still ! far yonder gleaming,
　　Shines my Saviour's glorious cross.

Oh, very beautiful is life,
　　And earthly flowers are passing fair :
But lift, oh lift me up to heaven,
　　And let me rest forever there.

There, no care shall plough its furrows ;
　　There, no sin shall blur my heart ;
There, in blessed choirs of angels,
　　I shall sing a humble part.

Lift me higher !   Lift me higher !
　　Friends of earth, no tears for me !
From temptation, sin, and sorrow,
　　Let me be forever free !

Ah ! I hear my Saviour call me !
　　Clad in heavenly robes of white ;
He will lift me higher, higher,
　　From this world of storm and night.

Lift me higher !   Lift me higher !
　　Farewell earthly friends I love.
Lift me higher !   Lift me higher !
　　To that better world above !

" Lift me higher !"   And our darling
　　Gently closed her wearied eyes ;
And her spirit, lifted higher,
　　Reached its home beyond the skies.

She is sleeping, and white marble
    This inscription only bears :
" Our lost flower—thirteen summers—
    Lifted higher"—than life's cares.

SILVERY FOUNTAIN.

SILVERY Fountain! soft and clear
    Falls thy murmuring on mine ear ;
And thy flowing ever brings
The memory that round me clings
                Of long ago.

Resting on thy brink so oft,
Mingling with thy music soft,
I have heard words, sad and sweet,
Words no mortal can repeat
                In days of yore.

When thy shining streamlet fell,
Ere it reached the crystal shell

My head would catch the glittering gleam,
And diamonds with my gold would beam
                    Like stars on night.

In waking dreams, with half-closed eyes,
I've seen fair forms from thee arise,
And wondered were they beings of earth,
With fairy forms, yet mortal birth,
                    Or rays of light.

I felt that angel ones were near,
And hoping, knowing, they would hear—
My heart's thoughts to my lips would rise,
And prayers be wafted to the skies,
                    On wings of love.

Ah, speak again !   No unknown tongue
Was thine to me, when I was young ;
Fain would I linger near thy side
And die, that those I love might guide
                    My soul above.

CRAZED.

No rest ! no rest on this bleak earth for me ;
    A thousand fancies flit across my brain ;
Dim phantoms of the shadowy past I see—
    I know, oh God ! I know I am insane.

Deep in my breast the secret I will hide—
    To those who love me 'twould give bitter pain:
Foes would rejoice should evil ere betide,
    And 'tis an awful curse to be insane.

Ho ! ho ! a light ! I say, my wife, a light !
    This heavy darkness crushes my poor heart ;
And, darling, sit beside my bed to-night—
    Thy kind words comfort to my soul impart.

Ah, do not start, when my deep groans you hear :
  I stagger, struck with agony so fell ;
See there ! see there ! 'tis gone ; you need not fear ;
  You cannot see the Devil's mystic spell.

I hear a footstep ! Halt ! I say, who's there ?
  The wind, you answer ; ah, I'm not insane !
You can't deceive me with your words so fair—
  There ! there ! I hear the sound approach again.

The light ! I say ! I tell you I will see—
  It is a thief, with murderous thought intent ;
You can't prevent me—but, ah, woe is me !
  Are you, too, on some hidden mischief bent ?

Forgive me, darling ; I did wildly rave ;
  I think I am a little crazed to-night.
Stay with me, pet-wife, you are good and brave ;
  The spell will pass with morning's dawning bright.

Press your soft hand upon my aching head—
    Weeping again ?   Why will you always weep ?
Your eyes their brightness with the tears will shed :
    There, good night, darling ! now, I fain would
        sleep.

NO LETTER.

" NO letter !" poor mother ! oh, well may'st
        thou weep,
    For thy noble and manly first-born
Is now sleeping peacefully death's dreamless sleep ;
    He shall never again see the morn.

" No letter !" and yet from his pocket they took,
    When they searched there to find out his name,
A missive unfinished in his Holy Book,
    All hopeful of glory and fame.

" In battle to-day our flag I'll uphold,
    And defend, though I lose my right arm ;
I am young, I have strength, and with courage
        am bold,
    With my life, I will shield it from harm.

" I must go, dear mother ! I hear the drums call,
　　And I will write more on the morrow."
Alas ! ere that day closed, the enemy's ball
　　To that mother bequeathed ceaseless sorrow.

No letter ! and sadly the wife turned away,
　　And crushed in her heart the great pain,
As God gave her patience, while day after day
　　She sought for the letter in vain.

" No letter !" your children are fatherless now ;
　　Bow in meekness to God's stern decree,
Your husband, with laurel wreaths twined round
　　　　his brow,
　　Is at rest in the land of the free.

" No letter !" sweet maiden, your lover so brave,
　　To his heart clasped your image and fell ;
Said he gloried to fill a poor soldier's grave,
　　For the country he loved so well.

To leave you alone was his only regret,

    In this sad world of sorrow and sin ;

But your grief he was hopeful you soon would

        forget,

    And sighing for what might have been.

" No letter !" dear sister, your brother is dead ;

    Alas ! he was shot in the battle ;

No sister's hand near to hold his cold head,

    With no one to hear the death-rattle.

Only those who have writhed 'neath the heart-

        crushing thought,

    And who live upon hope's brittle thread,

Can know the sad trial, with which life is fraught,

    Brings the longing to be with the dead.

THE TRYST.

I WAITED full two hours, or more,
 Beneath the old pine tree,
Where oft I've lingered twilight hours,
 Watching, my Love, for thee.

I waited till the shadows grew
 Like giants, grim and grey ;
I waited till night's coming chased
 The shadows far away.

I waited for, I knew not what ;
 But, oh, I waited there,
Hoping, perchance, some ray to find,
 To lighten my despair.

A year ago last May, I sat
    Beneath the old pine-tree ;
My tryst was not a broken one,
    For, Love, you came to me.

I waited, and my spirit called
    Thy spirit, Love, to me ;
No tryst was ever broken there
    Beneath the old pine-tree.

HOPE.

A S shines the sunbeam through dark clouds,
    Hope breaks the spirit's lowering shrouds
E'en as the morning dawns o'er night,
Hope sheds her radiant, golden light.

Like the soft dew to thirsting flower,
Hope e'er revives the soul's faint hour—
A soothing balm for every grief;
Hope, precious hope, finds sure relief.

The anchor of the tide-bound soul,
With breakers near, while billows roll
Around, about, but ne'er o'erwhelm,
With Hope the anchor, Faith the helm.

Hope, like the olden Shepherd's star,
Telleth her tidings from afar ;
And though earth's flowers fade and die,
Hope, Hope revives them in the sky.

AUTUMN THOUGHTS.

I, FROM my chamber-window, mark
    The dying of the year ;
The trees in red and green and gold,
    Show Autumn's progress sere ;
And soon, alas ! these richest tints
    Will change to sober brown ;
The trees of their bright garb bereft,
    Wear winter's sternest frown.

The warbling songster seeks in vain
    Some place to shield his wings,
And shivering on the bare cold oak,
    In piteous notes he sings.
The flowerets hide their frail bright heads
    Till winter shall be o'er,
Then at the first faint call of Spring,
    They show themselves once more.

The autumn rain is falling slow,
　　With chilling, solemn spell,
As if no brightness ever more
　　On this bleak earth shall dwell.
The dying of the day or year
　　With awe impress the mind ;
For though we know God's ways are right,
　　His mercies ever kind,—

We mortals seldom stop to think,
　　When brooding o'er the night,
How quickly day will dawn again,
　　And Spring again bloom bright ;
And at the end of life's short path
　　The aged should remember,
Eternal Spring-time dawneth bright
　　Soon after bleak December.

"THAT GLOVE."

WHY cherish thus the senseless thing?
　　Do memories around it cling
　　　Of joys long past?
Or does it speak of present bliss?
Do sweet last word, or parting kiss,
　　　Charms o'er it cast?

Now were it but a thing with life,
In which were earthly passions rife,
　　　Then I could see
Why you should press it to your heart,
Nor let it from your hand depart—
　　　It cannot flee.

You touch it, and you are unmann'd—
I hold it passive in my hand—
    No thrill of love
Shoots through my veins ; you bow before it,
The loving slave of her who wore it—
    That white kid glove !

You fought for freedom.   You were brave,
I grant it.   Even now you rave
    Of subjugation.
Yet you are subject of a queen,
Whose power greater is, I ween,
    Than Yankee nation.

Yes, e'en the touch of her small hand
Is equal to a stern command,
    Because you love.
You walk submissive in her band,
And when you cannot hold her hand,
    You hold her glove.

I do not judge thee—go thy way.
I have a glove—(what can I say?)
    And I adore it.
Ah ! often in the hours for sleep,
I kiss the glove, and sadly weep
    For one who wore it.

WAIL OF THE DIVORCED.

H OW can I give thee up, my child, my dearest,
   earliest born,
While fond hopes are 'round thee clustered, like
   bright clouds o'er morning's dawn ?
No, I will not leave thee, darling ; thou at least
   shall never say
That no tender hand did guide thee through the
   cares of childhood's day.

My child ! when first thy mother heard thy feeble,
   first-born wail,
Love's tide came rushing through the heart, I
   thought encased in mail.
For the few years of my young life had been scenes
   of mirth and woe,
For I grasped the pleasures, darling, grasped them,
   ere I let them go !

E'en the brightest days of summer have their sun-
    shine and their showers ;
And the piercing thorn will wound us, as we pluck
    the fairest flowers ;
But the perfume of the flowers makes us glory in
    the pain,
And exulting in the sunshine, we forget the chilling
    rain.

I know 'twould break my aching heart to leave
    thee, precious one !
How can they brand me with a curse—what have
    I ever done ?
I know that I have never sent a sister down to
    shame,
By casting blots of foulest sin upon a snow-white
    name.

Have charity, have charity, my child, for every sin—
For the sore temptation, darling, may all-powerful
    have been ;

And always lend a helping hand to those who
    chance to fall ;
Forgive, forget, be ready to obey your Saviour's
    call.

Learn, learn, my child, and ne'er forget, learn
    while thou art still young,
That he will have the truest friends, who bridleth
    his tongue.
Speak well of all, if aught you know of evil, or
    of ill ;
Deep in thy bosom let it rest, and keep the scandal
    still.

My baby, should you ever choose a partner for
    this life,
Oh, darling, ever strive to be a fond, devoted wife ;
And never let thy husband's name be spoken but
    in praise ;
For some will, if you let them, sadly misconstrue
    his ways.

Seek not happiness in pleasure, for the dregs of
  every cup
Are so bitter, darling, bitter, as we quaff the
  latest sup !
And never seek, my child, to win the laurel wreath
  of fame,
Unless thou hast a heart to bear the world's taunts,
  even shame.

Kind, noble, generous, they will give thy sister to
  me, dear :
But I must leave thee, child, and seek a home
  away from here.
Ah ! I defy them to the last ; they shall not part
  us, child
And thy mother's hand shall rear thee—rear thee,
  pure and undefiled !

May the fond prayers of thy mother prove a love-
  protecting shield
From each sorrow, and each harrowing care, that
  life doth ever yield.

And may the hand of love, my child, pluck thorns
    from thy bright flowers ;
And may'st thou find a home at last in heaven's
    celestial bowers.

THE OPIUM-EATER.

[Before taking a dose.]

LIFE'S pathway to me is dreary;
  I am ill, and cold, and weary;
Would my lonely walk were done,
And my heavenly race begun!

Once all things to me were bright,
Things that now seem dark as night:
Is the darkness all within?
Dark without from inward sin?

The present dark; eyes dim with age
Can see no joy, save memory's page.
The present, future, ne'er can be
Bright as the past they once did see.

My hair is turning quite grey now ;
I see some wrinkles on my brow ;
My teeth—they must be failing too,—
And corns are growing in my shoe.

I muffle up my aching face,
And pray from pangs a moment's grace.
Ah ! now the misery seeks my head—
Would I were with the pangless dead !

There is a cure for pain and grief—
Come, Opium, come to my relief !
Soothed by thy influence, I shall find
A moment's rest, and peace of mind.

[*After taking a dose.*]

Ah ! now I sit in bowers of bliss,
Soothed by an angel's balmy kiss !
Delicious languor o'er me stealing
Is now my only sense of feeling.

The breath of flowers perfumes the air ;
The forms around are—oh, so fair !
The once cold air seems warm and bright,
And I, too, seem a being of light.

My hair is not so very grey—
Some dye will take that hue away ;
A little powder shall, I vow,
Hide the small wrinkles on my brow.

My teeth are sound—I feel no pain—
Their slight ache was but sign of rain ;
And then the twinging of my feet
Was nothing but a dream, a cheat.

To me, the night, though dark, seems day,
Colored by Hope's most beauteous ray :
No sorrow hence shall give me pain—
I know I'll never weep again !

LITTLE BELL.

EVENING came, a child was missing,
    Where she was, we could not tell,—
Hiding, thought we, just for mischief ;
    Full of fun was little Bell.

Soon we found the little darling,
    Hiding in a grassy dell ;
All alone ?   No, gentle angels
    Kept safe guard o'er little Bell.

Her sweet chubby cheek was resting
    On her little dimpled hands ;
While her sunny curls were shining
    On her brow, in golden bands.

Silken eyelids softly closing
    O'er the dancing eyes of blue,
Kept the envious stars from seeing
    Earth can have her diamonds too.

A stick for gun and flag of bonnet
    By her on the grass-bed lay ;
Ah, poor Bell, our cruel warfare
    Came to naught, like children's play.

Naught, alas ! but blood and sorrows,
    By each hearth a vacant place ;
Years of joy can not redeem us
    As a nation from disgrace.

Gentle be thy life's sweet slumbers ;
    Purity in thy heart dwell ;
Every blessing rest upon thee—
    Is my prayer for little Bell.

WEARINESS.

A H, is there no, no place on earth
　　Where weary souls can rest ?
Are none who spring from mortal birth
　　With perfect bliss e'er blest ?

Or shall we be forever longing—
　　Be with wants and wishes filled ;
Craving things to earth belonging,
　　Not the things that God hath willed ?

Oh ! how weary, weary, weary,
　　And how long doth seem the day,
When too sad, and lone and dreary,
　　Plod we on our toilsome way ?

With not one, not one to love us,
　　How can we of bliss e'er dream ?
Of the blissful heaven above as
　　Can we ever catch a gleam ?

Can we long endure such sorrow
　　Without longing for the day—
Praying God that ere the morrow
　　We may pass from earth away ?

Is there even one, a mortal,
　　Who content with life's sad store
Would retreat from heaven's blest portal,
　　And return to earth once more ?

ONLY A BLUSH.

ONLY a blush ! O'er the cheek it swept,
　　In a tint, but a shade more bright,
While over the forehead the soft glow crept,
　　Like Aurora's roseate light.

Only a blush ! 'Twas a single word
　　That the heart's deep fountain woke,
And in turbulent gushes, its depths were stirred,
　　For the lips were loved that spoke.

Only a blush ! Yet the glow revealed
　　That she loved him, and with pride
In the armor of many a conquest steel'd,
　　He lingered near her side,

And breathed into her credulous ear,
    In the whim of an idle hour,
Vows never forgotten by those who hear
    When subjected to Love's cruel power.

Only a blush ! Long it lingered there
    And assumed a hectic token,
When the vows that woke it had vanished in air,
    And the maiden's heart was broken.

A KISS.

A KISS? Pray tell me, what is in a kiss,
That it should be the ultimate of bliss?
I've tried it, and in vain ; I cannot see
Why so much sought for a mere kiss should be.

I wish I knew wherein lies the delight,
The smacking part ! What's in that to excite ?
Or drinking souls from lips, as lovers do—
Ah, let me see—and did I try that too ?

I have convinced myself it must be good,
When people kiss each other as they should ;
A mouth with rosy lips and a moustache
Together met, knock reason " *all to smash.*"

KINDNESS.

ONE single word of heartfelt kindness,
    Oft is worth a mine of gold,—
Yet how oft, we, in our blindness,
    The most precious wealth withhold.

Like soft dews on thirsting flowers,
    It revives the drooping heart ;
And its magical blest showers
    Is the soul's best healing art.

Oh ! however sad and lonely
    Life's dark, sterile path may be,
One, one single kind word only
    Causeth all its gloom to flee.

How can we know of the troubles
    That must rack another's soul,
All must know that empty bubbles
    Of Life's cares o'er all heads roll.

Then forgiving and forgetting,
    Let for aye the kind word fall,
Only our own sins regretting
    With a charity for all.

Then this life will be a pleasure,
    When we all speak words of love,
For we know our earthly measure
    Will be more than filled above.

CHILD LIFE.

L IKE the cadence of an old love song,
　　Borne on a zephyr's wings along,
Fading
　　　　and dying,
　　　　　　　　Then sounding again,
Touching the heart with its mournful strain,
Tearing my soul from its worldly strife,
Came a dream or vision of life, child-life.

Methought the heart of a child stood bare,
And I saw all human passions there,
Urging
　　　　and surging
　　　　　　　　Like waters grand,
Hurled by the mælstrom's mighty hand,
While the billows dashed with a sullen sound,
And scattered the foaming spray around.

'Twas a tiny seed in its embryo state,
Yet I saw there the germs of love and hate—
Loving

   and hating !

      Together they stood,
Strange that the evil should rest by the good !
Oh ! would that to mortals was granted the meed
To cherish the flower, but pluck out the weed !

Faith, Hope and Charity, all were there,
Ambition, revenge, dark revenge, and despair,
Doubting

   and wondering,

      I touched a small sore,
And the heart of the child was enveloped in gore.
'Twas a slight disappointment that brought forth
   the blood,
For a sire's broken promise disturbed the deep
   flood.

Ah ! I covered my eyes to shut out the sad sight,
For the face of the child was as dark as the night
Craving

      and praying

          That knowledge to find
A rest for the weary, a balm for the mind.
With Faith I looked up, and the child's face was
      fair ;
Hope's flower had blossomed through blood and by
      prayer.

And as the dream-vision was passing away,
Through the deep silence reigning I heard a voice say,
Receive

      and believe,

          Thou, a mother of youth,
Oh ! doubt not this vision, thou knowest its truth !
Thou knowest that virtues and passions are rife
In the beautiful morning of life, child-life.

Beware how thou touchest its heart cords wrong,
For the virtues are weak and the vices are strong.
Gently

    and tenderly,

        Wake the sweet strain,
Touch pleasure and peace, and no discord will reign.
Thou hast seen, oh my daughter, that each child
    of earth
Doth emulate manhood, yes, e'en at its birth.

Then deal with it lovingly, let the dream last,
When comes a deep sorrow, the child-life is past.
Softly

    and sweetly—

        Like light falling rain,
Then dying away as Æolian strain,
The dream-vision vanished, I heard still the voice,
Group no longer in darkness, in thy knowledge
    rejoice.

I woke, and the sun newly born, grand and bright,
Had flooded my room, and my soul with its light.

EVANISHINGS.

"DARLING, how long before this breath
will cease?
How long before my soul shall have sweet peace?
I am so weary, that I fain would rest,
Would rest forever on my Saviour's breast.

Ah ! let me gaze once more upon the earth,
So gay, so bright, so full of joy and mirth.
The song-birds sing, and bright flowers bloom for me,
And night's pure stars shine on me lovingly :

Earth is all brightness, still I fain would go
Where all is real, where joy ne'er turns to woe,
Where this frail body will be free from pain,
Where we shall meet, no more to part again.

Sallie H. Perine

'Tis dark here, father ! Oh, weep not for me,
For Heaven is light through all Eternity.
In the pure garland of her Saviour's love
Your bud will shed her fragrance far above.

Oh, mother ! Think I've only gone before,—
My sisters ! That we soon shall meet once more.
Weep not for me ! my heart is passing light,
I'll rest to-morrow robed in spotless white.

Speak louder ! for my earthly senses fail—
Terrestrial things before my dim sight pale.
Celestial visions meet my fading sight ;
I hear sweet music in the realms of light.

And thou, beloved, who art near my side—
But one short month and I had been thy bride.
How can I leave thee ? 'Tis my Saviour's voice,
He would espouse me—fainting heart, rejoice.

Farewell to all, a long and last farewell !

The angels call me where immortals dwell !

With a sweet smile she breathed her latest breath,

And thus our darling triumphed over death.

LIFE FOR A LIFE.

'TIS but a phantom of the weary brain,
    An image wrought by sleepless nights of
      pain—
I know 'tis false, as false as earth can be,
Thy hand, my son, from blood of man is free.

Ah! ha! Thou shrinkest, oh, my son! my son!
If thou art guilty then am I undone!
Still thou art mine, a widow's only child;
Some subtle serpent has thy heart beguiled.

Plead for thee, boy? ay, give my life for thine—
A mother's love is holy, pure, divine.
I will away, to Cromwell will I hie,
And save thee, boy, ay, save or with thee die!

With brow unbent, grim Cromwell stood
      Within the Council Hall,
Vouchsafing scarce the slightest glance
      Upon the form to fall
Of her who pleaded for the boon
      Most precious earth can give.
"Life for a life," old Cromwell said.
      She pleaded, let him live.
No eloquence so powerful as eloquence of love,
It melts the frozen fountain and the hardest heart
      can move.
Let me go back, the woman cried, to happy days
      of yore !
That wayward boy you doom to death is a young
      child once more.
See, see his bright and sunny curls now cradled on
      my breast !
Again I sing sweet lullaby and soothe my babe to
      rest.

Sleep, darling, sleep,
 Thy mother's near,
Sleep, baby, sleep,
 Thou knowest no fear.
Sleep, baby, sleep,
 Upon my breast ;
Sleep, darling, sleep,
 Sweet be thy rest.

Cromwell, your heart is hard, they say, but you
 have children too ;
War's tide may turn, you too may plead for some
 life dear to you.
Then let your better nature act, oh, let my son go
 free,
And daily prayers by me and mine shall soar aloft
 for thee.

His features soften ; does his heart relent towards
 my son ?
I will another picture draw, then is my pleading
 done :

See, Cromwell, see, upon the lawn, my curly headed
      boy,
He knows not he is fatherless, my blessed, only
      joy.

See how he gambols ! how can he know aught of
      my deep grief ?
Tears, scalding tears pour from mine eyes, to give
      my heart relief.
Ah, now he rushes to my side, and wipes away a
      tear :
Oh, weep not, mother, for my sire, for, mother, I
      am here.

Soon, very soon I'll be a man ; and then I'll work
      for you—
But I am little now, mamma, and what can
      children do ?
Now all forgetful of my grief, he playful leaves my
      side—
You cannot slay my only son, my darling and my
      pride !

" Life for a life," again he said, yet hurried a tear
     to hide ;

Then gazing from the casement low, his cheek
     flushed in its pride.

The pleader's eye had followed his, to where his
     mother stood,

Well might the conqueror be proud of one so pure
     and good !

The doomed man's mother grasped his arm ; thy
     mother, Cromwell, see !

Perchance the time may come, stern man, she may
     thus plead for thee.

" Vengeance is mine, I will repay," hath said the
     Lord thy King—

Spare, spare my child, and blessings rare upon thy
     household bring.

" Life for life,"—then spare my son, and, Cromwell,
     let me die ;

A mother's love will brave all earth, and even
     death defy.

The warrior in his fancy saw his mother's bended
    knee,
Tearing her gray hairs in her grief, yet all unheard
    her plea.

His stern heart softened, and his eye betrayed the
    pitying gleam
Which brightened his harsh, stern old face, like a
    celestial beam.
Go, woman, go, thy prayer is heard, and thy dear
    son shall live !
This time shall mercy, justice rule, and I for once
    forgive.

APPLE DUMPLINGS.

BY REQUEST.

GAZE not upon my outside, friend,
    With scorn or with disgust—
Judge not, until you condescend
    To look beneath the crust.

Rough and unsightly is my shell,
    But you just dues will render ;
And to the world the truth will tell,
    And say my heart is tender.

The young may scorn my olden ways,
    With their new-fashioned notions ;
The old the insult soon repays
    By claiming double portions.

'Tis true, like modern Misses, gay,
     The truth is sad, distressing !
But I must now say out my say—
     I need a little *dressing !*

My sauce, my rich apparel, hides
     My ugly form from sight ;
The goodness of my heart, besides,
     Will always come to light.

Then judge not by the surface, dear ;
     Look deeper at the heart :
Above the faults of earth appear
     Beneath the better part.

LIFE.

LIFE? What is life but fleeting bliss,
As transient as a lover's kiss,
Or like a flower
Of beauty and of fragrance rare
Which blooms, then vanishes in air,
In one short hour.
Unlike the flower, the soul will bloom,
Transplanted far above earth's gloom,
By God's vast power.

Life? What is life? 'Tis but a dream
Of weal or woe, a lightning's gleam,
That fades away.
Yet leaves its impress on the mind—
Some tie that memory will bind

With Love's warm ray :
Or, like the fiery subtle light,
The thoughts of its destroying blight
     May last for aye.

Life ?   What is life ?   A morning mist,
Which vanishes when e'er 'tis kissed
     By Sol's rays bright ;
'Tis but a silver-tinted cloud,
Which floats so beautifully proud
     In realms of light.
But gaze beneath the silver crest,
You find, deep buried in its breast,
     Storms dark as night.

Life ?   What is life ?   Hopes, bright hopes
     wrecked ;
Desire curbed, ambition checked,
     By earthly scorn.
Vows, sacred vows, too lightly spoken ;
Hearts filled with joy, neglected, broken,

'Till at each dawn
The victim sighs for death's release—
For with death will all troubles cease,
And peace is born.

Life ?   What is life ?   A heaving sea,
Which take us to Eternity ;
Its billows, Time
Upon whose waves our barks are mann'd,
By God's all-powerful command,
To other clime,—
Perchance our goal is land of night,
Or we may take the form of light
In realms sublime.

Life ? what is life ? that we should grieve
The transient pomps of earth to leave,
When we must see
That flowers bloom to fade away—
That joys last not, for e'en a day.

That pleasures flee :
We know that in the land above
We shall redeemed by hand of love
        All perfect be.

Then gladly should our souls rejoice
To hear our dear Redeemer's voice
        Call us away.
Glad to exchange this land of night—
This land of sorrow and of blight—
        For endless day ;
Where, clothed in robes of spotless white,
We'll live in realms of boundless light,
        For aye, and aye.

THE SIGNAL GUN.

SOFTLY now the day is dawning,
　　Song-birds sing the lays of morning ;
Al else around is calm and still,
Except the picket on the hill.

Now where once the morning breeze
Sweetly floated through the trees ;
Grim earth-batteries rear on high
Their ghastly heads up to the sky.

From morning's light to evening shades
We dwell in dread of martiral raids ;
With faith we trust protecting power
Will shelter us in this dark hour.

Listen ! now the signal-gun
Tells the picket's work is done ;
No more will he watch and wait—
Stands he now at heaven's gate.
Yes, the picket's race is run,
And his heavenly life begun.

ALL ALONE.

AND shall we ever seek in vain,
　　In this cold world of ours,
The love of kindred heart to gain
　　To rouse our latent powers ?
Or shall our hearts forever mourn
　　　　　　All alone ?

Upon the silvery moon I gaze
　　And the bright gems of night ;
And from their loving, tender rays,
　　My soul imbibes God's light.
Why to me is that radiance borne
　　　　　　All alone ?

I *feel* each gentle, soothing word—
　　The perfume of the flower—
The thrilling music of the bird—
　　The twilight's quiet hour :
And sigh to think these joys mine own,
　　　　　　All alone.

Once in my early youth I thought
　　That answered was my prayer ;
Alas ! experience soon taught
　　'Twas but a dream so fair :
In heaven, blest heaven, I shall not mourn
　　　　　　All alone !

UPON RECEIPT OF A POUND OF COFFEE IN 1863.

THE sight of the coffee was good for sore eyes,
    For I have not learned yet its worth to
        despise ;
I welcomed each grain as I culled with care o'er,
And in fancy increased it to ten thousand more.

I put it on fire, and stirred round and round,
Then took it off gently when it was quite browned ;
When cool I proceeded to fill up my mill,
And ground up a boiling with very good will.

I measured three spoons full, you see, for us three—
The old Lady Lane, my Grand-mother and me ;
I added some water, then put it to boil,
And stood close by, watching, for fear it might spoil.

I put cream and sugar in three of our cups,
Then poured out our coffee, and took some good sups.
I thought of the Turk, sitting on his curled knees,
And was sure that our coffee, his Lordship would
     please.

It spoiled me, and now I'm beginning to think,
When that coffee gives out, what the mischief I'll
      drink ;
I must get some coffee—beg, borrow, or steal—
For after that Java, I can't drink parched meal !

Thus down to the bottom we drank your good
      health !
May God shower o'er you of blessings a wealth ;
May you never want for good coffee and tea—
And, friend, in your buying, remember poor me !

MRS. MYRICK'S LECTURE.

YOU know, dear, that this vicious world is
      ever prone to see,
Most glaring faults and blemishes, in even purity ;
And thus, my dear, a shade of black will much the
      darker show,
Should it chance to be embedded in the virgin
      white of snow.

The modest floweret of the wood that's born to
      blush unseen,
May all its simple defects hide with its own veil
      of green ;
But woe betide the stately rose, the pride of the
      parterre,
Should but the canker-spot of life upon its leaves
      appear.

The rose's heart, for that is hid, may with the
     blight corrode ;
Have faults, but ever hide them well, for that is
     a-lá-mode ;
Should you but say that you have sinned—that you
     are but a mortal—
The world, amazed, will scorning cry, " she'll ne'er
     see heaven's portal !"

The brittle glass of character will have stains on it
     cast
By malice of the slanderous world, for simple faults,
     long past ;
No matter how much tempted, or how pure your
     heart has been,
You're wicked, in the last degree, if scandal knows
     your sin.

Thank God ! repentant sinners are not judged by
     those of earth,
Or they would never be redeemed by an immortal
     birth.

Ah ! He, when the last trump shall sound, " who
    doeth all things well,"
Will wipe our sorrowing tears away, and pains of
    anguish quell.

See the flaw in this bright diamond ; were it but a
    thing of glass,
A much larger flaw, unnoticed, would before the
    world's eye pass ;
Gaze in the clearest waters, rocks and blemishes
    you spy,
That in less clearer streamlets would be hidden
    from your eye.

Be not offended now, my dear, at counsel from a
    friend,
Who blessings on thy youthful head, would daily,
    hourly send.
Deep in your heart your secrets keep ; to enemies
    be civil ;
And oh, be careful, and avoid appearances of evil.

TO FANNIE.

WRITE to thine eyes?   Why, my poor pen
  Quails at the unequal task ;
I fear you don't appreciate
  The mighty boon you ask.

Thine eyes, I know, oh ! beautiful !
  True poets would inspire ;
But, dear, you should remember, that
  I've not a poet's fire.

But still at thy request I call
  My sleeping muse to me,
To write a sonnet to thine eyes—
  Would it were worthy thee !

Tender and loving, soft and pure,
    They pierce the heart of man ;
And with the aid of Cupid's darts,
    Maim all the hearts they can.

Bright as the stars in yonder sky,
    They shine for all on earth :
So sad in sorrow, glad in joy,
    And sparkling in their mirth.

They, like the eyes of the gazelle,
    Gaze fondly where you love ;
And who receives such gaze, esteems
    Them angels from above.

Bright as the light of long-sought home
    To pilgrims o'er earth's way,
Whose footsteps sore, have wandered far,
    Through weary year and day.

The light of love, the light of truth,
    From thy soft eyes e'er beam ;
And from thy heart, so kind and true,
    A host of virtues gleam.

Now if this sonnet, Fannie, dear,
    Were written by a lover,
A thousand charms no doubt he'd see,
    That I cannot discover.

I AM WEARY, MOTHER,

I AM weary, Mother, and I fain would rest
   Beside thee, in the cold and silent tomb—
The rayless pathways of a life unblest,
   Are dark, beside the brightness of death's gloom.

I place my hand upon the marble white
Above thee, Mother, and it chills my frame ;
Yet 'tis not cold as hearts which take delight
In casting stains upon a once fair name.

Few summers, Mother, smiled above thy head ;
Ere thou wast chilled by breath of Azael's wing,
Love, flowers and sunshine brightness o'er thee
     shed,
But naught had power immortal life to bring.

My life has been one checkered scene of woe ;
True, Spring and Summer flowers 'round me cast—
But ah, they faded, like all things below—
Bloomed but a moment, and like dreams, were past.

Why didst thou leave me, Mother ? thy frail child
Had not the strength to guide her bark alone ;
Full many a soul by false lights are beguiled,
But few are safely o'er life's breakers borne.

Ah ! I have erred, my Mother ; but my sin
Upon Him rests, whose blood all guilt redeems !
My heart was weak—but who is pure within ?
What heart untouched by sin's dread, seething
        gleams ?

But, Mother, I have left me some bright hours—
I revel 'mid the Barmacidian feast !
I cull imagination's fairest flowers ;
I live again, with Shepherds in the East.

Oft Cleopatra's magic wand I wield
O'er Anthony and Julius Cæsar's reign—
With Sheba's queen, to Solomon I yield—
And, with fair Ruth, I glean the scanty grain.

With Beatricia Canci now I sigh,
The helpless victim of a Father's sin ;
In loathsome dungeons, with her prey to die,
And weeping, think of joys which might have been

By Eloise, within the convent cell,
I listen for my Abelard's loved voice,
Whose every cadence, ah ! I know full well,
Whose softest footsteps make my heart rejoice.

Is it a sin to dream ? to live once more
Among remembered nations of the past—
To recall those who've only gone before,
And live beyond the reach of earth's rude blast ?

The future, Mother, hath bright charms for me ;
Not on this earth, but in my home above,
Where from temptation, sin, and sorrow free,
I'll see once more the dear ones that I love.

LIGHT IN DARKNESS.

MOTHER, for months a mist has been before
    me,
   And I have sought, in memory, to bind
All objects loved, ere darkness gathered o'er me,
   For in my heart, I felt I would be blind.

I am so young, my Mother, that my sorrow
   Is fraught with bitter anguish of despair;
How can I bear to think, that each to-morrow
   Will robe in darkness all earth's beauties rare!

I feel a sunbeam, Mother, resting on me;
   I take the omen to my breaking heart—
For thy sweet voice, thy loving hand upon me,
   Will to thy son bright rays of light impart.

'Tis said that beauties, Mother, grow still fairer,
    When looked upon through vista of past years,
And that joy's paintings seem still brighter, rarer,
    Their colors set by sorrow's briny tears.

On memory's tablet, Mother, I have flowers
    More beautiful than artist's cherished gems—
And bright tipped clouds of twilight quiet hours,
    More prized by me than countless diadems.

And trees of Autumn, with their hues e'er changing,
    And then the gentle budding green of Spring
Will keep my thoughts from ever, ever ranging
    To leafless boughs that winter's blasts e'er bring

And I have faces passing sweet, too, Mother—
    More holy than Corregio's fair saint ;
Yes, I have drawn thy image, sister, brother,
    And thine too, Mother, without earthly taint.

And, Mother, now too surely I am dreaming :
    Sweet Lily's eyes will soon become my light,—
No, 'tis no dream, and earth with joy is teeming,
    For Lily promised to be mine last night.

THE HUMMING-BIRD.

I ENTERED my parlor one bright summer morn,
    My vases with flowers, sweet flowers to adorn.
In arranging the curtains, there fell on my head
A dear little humming-bird, dead—quite dead !

I pressed the poor darling so close to my heart,
And thought that I felt a slight flutter, a start !
Could I but restore it to life, how divine,
How sweet, how delicious a joy would be mine !

I rushed to the garden and placed its long mouth
In the sweet honey-suckle which blooms in the South;
I saw that the humming-bird drew a long breath,
As it tasted the nectar that saved it from death !

The minutes flew past, yet I staid in the bower,
And moved my poor birdling from flower to flower ;
At last, with a sweet strain of grateful heart's
        praise,
It flew upward, far upward, beyond my eyes' gaze.

Thus when you, dear children, are dying in sin—
When all is a void and an aching within—
Drink deep of the nectar of God's holy love,
And your souls will be wafted to mansions above.

THE SOLDIER BOY'S DREAM

A SOLDIER boy lay dreaming
  In his lonely prison cell,
While the stars above were gleaming,
  And their lustre on him fell.
His dreams were bright, angels of light
  Were hovering o'er his head ;
'Twas day in night, the spirit's sight,
  The living of sleep's dead.

On wings of love his soul was borne
  By the celestial band,
Where he no longer mourned alone,
  To his home in Southern land.

He roved in bowers, amid sweet flowers
    Of every kind, and shade,—
The mock-bird's note thrilled from its throat,
    And music filled the glade.

His noble sire, with silver hair,
    Again stood by his side ;
His saintly mother breathed a prayer
    For this her son, her pride.
And yet again, joy deep brings pain !
    His Katy meets him there—
Stands by his side, his promised bride ;
    Sweet Katy, pure and fair.

Again he cools his fever'd brain
    With water soft and clear,
Whose murmuring, like distant rain,
    Falls soothing on his ear.
And now a stroke the silence broke,
    The wood-bird seeks his prey,—
Ah ! 'tis not dreams, the daylight gleams,
    The wood-bird's strokes still stay.

The boy sprang to his window small,
    Gazed on the passing night—
A new-made gallows, grim and tall,
    Loomed to his eager sight :
In his despair, he tore his hair,
    And cursed the craven nation,
Who for but hate, made death his fate—
    Noble retaliation !

A soft hand touched the stricken'd boy,
    And an Æolian voice
Bade him, in accents full of joy,
    To follow, and rejoice !
On by the guards, the sleeping guards,
    They flew like silent death,
Without a sound the gate they found,
    Scarce drawing e'en a breath.

Now the dread danger all is o'er ;
    He turned to thank his guide ;
He gazed again once more, once more—
    No one stood near his side.

Celestial light dawned o'er his night,
    Earth seemed with glory bound,—
Filled him with joy, the blissful joy
    Of LIBERTY, new found.

MINE.

HER eyes are bright as sparkling stars,
    And as the violet blue ;
In them celestial beauty lies,
    The soul-light flashing through.

No painter, how e'er great his skill,
    Can imitate her hair ;
Naught save a sunset sea of gold
    Had ever shade so rare.

The lilies with pale roses blend,
    And melt upon her cheek—
Her carmine lips disclose seed pearls,
    When e'er they ope to speak !

Her tiny ear, like sea-side shell,
    Pink-ting'd, of perfect mould,
A moment gleams, then disappears,
    Lost in the sea of gold.

Ah, should you see my birdie blithe,
    In some lone sylvan dell,
You'd think she was a fairy child,
    Made mortal by a spell.

Her voice ! ah, never tropic bird
    Could trill so sweet a glee ;
Nor is the sad Æolian harp
    So full of melody.

My birdie speaks, no earthly strain
    Could thus my spirit move,
For her sweet notes pierce through my heart,
    And thrill the cords of love.

For this fair child, this fairy bright,
  So nearly being divine,
To me is sunshine, hope and life—
  For she is mine, all mine !

MISTLETOE.

ON yonder oak, upon its lordliest height,
    Is fastened the destroying parasite ;
His mighty arms caress his fawning foe,
And yield their life-sap to the mistletoe.

Through bark, through wood, the fatal roots
    extend ;
The parasitic verdure seems a friend,
O'erspreading the gnarled trunk with livelier
    green—
Alas ! decay, and death soon end the scene !

First dies the oak, and then the parasite
Cannot survive its royal patron's blight ;
And when I look abroad among mankind,
Close semblance, and fit moral do I find.

God feared that poor, weak mortals here below
By chance might be too fond of earth's vain show
In hopes to draw our hearts from earth to heaven,
The monster jealousy to us was given.

Search where you may, this wide, wide world around,
The green-eyed thing in every house is found ;
In truth, it bitters every sweet of life,
And creates discord between man and wife.

To some it wears the winning garb of love,
And seems as sweet as any cooing dove :
Look closely, and perchance you can discover
The thing has other form than that of lover.

To sisters, brothers, fathers, mothers too,
As friend it goes, and seems so kind and true,
That they would fain believe all that it says,
And take, for pattern, its own *noble* ways.

Like mistletoe, it seems so green and bright,
At first you'd view it with unfeigned delight ;
Examine it again, and you will see
Its nature with its looks does not agree.

For jealousy from out the tree of love
Its verdure draws, and like the plant above,
The roots, instead of dying, as they should
With age, become embedded in the wood.

And thus it lives, long, weary months and years,
And causes sorrow, guilt, and heartfelt tears,—
The boisterous winds of sorrow bear the seed,
And plant on other trees the loathsome weed.

Alas ! in mercy sent, no tender hand
Can take this parasite from our good land ;
It stays, and from its birth-place never hies,
Until it kills the tree, and then it dies.

FAMILY PORTRAITS.

FIVE buds were on the parent tree,
　　But God took one away ;
" This flower will be too fair," said He,
　　" Upon this earth to stay."

And now, by His own throne above,
　　Our bud is blooming fair ;
Twined in the garland of His love,
　　Our Prince is proud to wear.

A smaller bud now groweth there,
　　Whose red we just descry—
A blithesome child, with silken hair,
　　Gay as a butterfly.

With joy and gladness for her dower,
    And always on the wing,
She extracts sweets from every flower—
    For her, life has no sting.

    *   *   *   *   *

My Pet ! of all, I love *thee* best—
    Thou child of noblest mind,—
Who lov'st me more than all the rest,
    So generous, good and kind !

Sweet bud ! Thou'rt very fair to me,
    Unfolding day by day ;
From sorrow be thou ever free,
    On earth—long be thy stay !

    *   *   *   *   *

And still another openeth rare,
    Its petals now unclose,
More lovely far beyond compare
    Than any splendid rose.

Graceful her form, as willow tree,
    Her hair of sunny hue ;
Face fair as mortal face can be,
    Her eyes of heavenly blue.

Endowed with nature's every gift—
    With beauty, mind and health ;
Oh, may she never cast adrift
    Such store of Nature's wealth !

    *   *   *   *   *

Transplanted to another clime,
    The eldest bud hath bloomed ;
But cankered ere the opening time,
    Her life to sorrow doomed.

Once, thoughtless, happy, gay and bright,
    In life's young opening day,
'Till the fell frost, with glittering blight,
    Ate her young heart away.

Now she awaits her Saviour's voice,
    To kindly bid her come ;
Her broken heart can but rejoice
    To hear the summons home !

LINES TO AN OLD DRESS.

ALAS! the time has come, old dress,
    When you and I must part;
To say adieu, my valued friend,
    Is tearing heart from heart.

Long years have passed since thou wert new,
    Long years of war and crime;
But sight of thee to memory brings
    The olden golden time.

I'd braid my silken tresses smooth;
    Then cast thee o'er my form,
And press my hand upon my heart,
    To quell tumultuous storm.

For well I know whose eye would beam
    To see me thus arrayed ;
'Twas one whose gentle tender glance,
    His love for me betrayed.

Old dress, dost thou remember well
    That beauteous moon-light night,
When the hoped-for truth o'erwhelmed my heart,
    With a perfect blaze of light ?

How he clasped us to his heart, old dress,
    And he vowed beneath the stars,
That naught in heaven could us divide—
    'Twas registered by Mars.

Ah, the Gods but mocked us then, old dress,
    With a short, sweet dream of bliss,
That vanished, alas ! from our mortal sight,
    Like the dew at the sun's warm kiss.

In but a short year from then, old dress,
    That sudden gleam of light
Had passed away, and left me naught,
    But the darkness of midnight.

For Mars laughed at our arrogance,
    And he hurled his mighty dart,
And my love lies in the battle-field,
    And broken is my heart.

Ah, I cannot give thee up, old dress,
    For thy threads are links of chain,
That bind my memory to the past—
    To long gone joys and pain.

THE MOTHER'S LAMENT.

UPON THE LOSS OF HER CHILDREN'S PHOTOGRAPHS AT SEA.

HAST thou no mercy, wind, that thou should'st
    tear from me,
  All that is left me of my loved—my own ?
Thy hand is human, else it could not be
  With weight of sorrow in my poor heart borne.

Two clinging vines, trained by my erring hand,
  Two rose-buds, with their petals scarce
    unclosing—
See how they float, like tiny barks well manned,
  Now like a bird upon the wave reposing.

Mock me not, waves ! Why on your flirting spray,
  Toss ye my precious darlings to and fro ?
Oh ! save them, sailor, ere they pass away ;
  Their worth to me, no mortal's soul can know.

There ! see ye not their fairy brightness gleaming,
    Like stars upon the darkness of the night ?
See that fond smile upon each feature beaming ;
    Wave, can ye thus deprive my soul of light ?

On, on they fly ! too late ! the ocean cave
    Now claims among her jewels two rare gems,
Worth thousands such as Eastern monarchs crave,
    To form star-clusters in their diadems.

Whene'er I looked into those faces fair,
    Into those eyes of clear celestial blue,
I always prayed, and felt God heard my prayer,
    That for their sakes I might be good and true.

Now those fair faces and those eyes of blue,
    No more will daunt me with their pleading gaze;
The deep sea hides them from my reckless view,
    And unrebuked I'll walk in worldly ways.

No ! not unchecked ; when sin's allurements fair,
    Tempt me to err, with wily, subtle art,
I hear sweet voices in each breath of air,
    " See, mother, see ! thy children in thy heart."

Then keep my jewels, sea, and guard them well ;
    I care not, wind, for your revengeful rage ;
My babes are painted by love's mystic spell,
    In colors rare, upon fond memory's page.

TO FATHER.

MY father ! when I saw thee last,
    Thy noble, manly form,
Was unbent by the cares of time—
    Unshattered by life's storm.

The raven hair around thy brow
    Was scarcely tinged with gray—
While the bright lustre of thine eye
    Denied old age's sway.

Oft in my dreams I see thy face,
    As 'twas when last we met ;
If we should never meet again,
    Thy smile I'll ne'er forget.

My father, years have passed since then ;
  Aye, stern, heart-breaking years ;
And we have each been made to feel
  Life's sorrows, and life's tears.

Now, I am in my womanhood—
  They say, life's glorious page ;
And, father, I regret to think,
  That you have reached old age.

Grieve not, grieve not, for broken buds,
  They'll open in the sky ;
In bower of celestial light,
  They'll bloom, and never die.

Dear father, thou hast ever been
  To me, thy orphan child,
A father and a mother too,
  Kind, thoughtful, just and mild.

Then grant me, father, but this boon,
    Then will thy child be blest—
Let me watch o'er thy latest years,
    And lay thee down to rest.

I AM FASHION'S TOY.

LINES WRITTEN UPON SEEING A FASHIONABLY-DRESSED
LADY ASK A SERVANT FOR A FEW BLADES OF GRASS,
WHICH SHE PLACED UPON HER BOSOM.

OH ! give to me of the bright green leaves,
 For they tell me of the past ;
When I roved at will mid the golden sheaves—
And my heart it wildly, madly grieves,
 And it throbs so painfully fast,
As I think of the days of peace and joy
That forever are gone—I am fashion's toy.

Yes, the modeste decks my raven hair,
 In many a shape and coil—
And she dyes my cheek with the carmine rare,
And she makes my brow as the lily fair,

And they tell me, for beauty I can compare
      With the daughters of eastern soil ;
Yet, I sigh when I smile in my empty joy,
For I know, alas ! I am fashion's toy.

My form is stately, and full of pride—
And the high of the land linger near my side,
      Yet as they fawning bow,
My heart flows back on sweet memory's tide,
And I forget they are near my side,
      And the past seems to me now.
Then I dream of the sweets that could not cloy,
For a moment forget, I am fashion's toy.

Yes, this grass reminds me of long past hours,
      When in the woodland glen
I revelled 'mid song and birds and flowers,
And formed, with the evergreen, fairy bowers.
      Ah ! I was not lonely then ;
For he was with me, my pride, my joy—
He is dead to me now, I am fashion's toy.

Ah ! the hearts and the diamonds that lie at my
   feet—
Hearts are all hollow, and diamonds a cheat,
 Yet I cannot cast them away ;
I need much wealth for my life of deceit—
 Yes, I need it every day.
I must give to the poor, for that bliss doesn't cloy;
'Tis my only relief—I am fashion's toy.

And is there no end to this empty life ;
To this life of lip-smiles and a soul at strife ?
 Must it ever, ever last ?
Shall I look through the vista dim of years,
And see there naught but grief, sin, and tears ?
Ah ! these blades of grass for a moment brief,
O'erflood my soul with a sweet relief,
 And I live in the happy past.
In my dreams, I again am a maiden coy,
And I live o'er my life of love and joy—
Now, the dream is past. I am fashion's toy.

THE MAIL HAS COME.

NOW the bitter pangs of hope deferred
    O'er us no longer reign,—
But the very depths of our hearts are stirred
    With a still more poignant pain ;
And we sadly think of the lapse of years,
And our eyes grow dim with the unshed tears.

Where are the noble, the good, the brave,
    The father, husband, son ?
Can we bless the hand that the sorrow gave,
    And say, " Thy will be done ?"
Ah ! we sadly weep o'er their honored graves—
But we glory to think, that they died not slaves.

Yes, we scorn to yield to a tyrant's power :
    For oppression we despise ;
But ah, in the twilight's quiet hour,
    In bereaved hearts will arise
Fond thoughts of our kindred far away ;
And again Hope emits her bright diamond-like
      ray.

Now the mail has come ; in my trembling hand
    Many missives of love I hold ;
Northern brothers, such love is a stronger band
    Than our cotton, our slaves, your gold.
Now I open them, one by one, in dread
To hear from the living, and the dead.

Ah ! Ava Maria, mother mild,
    I thank thee for thy care ;
My father will see again his child,
    Thou hast hearkened to my prayer.
But his form is bent, and the hand of time
Has silvered his locks with its war and crime.

Why with bitter will mingle the sweets of earth?
　　Why with hope will come despair?
Why cherish sweet flowers, when at their birth,
　　We know that their beauties rare,
At the touch of stern winter's chilling blast,
Will vanish forever, like dreams of the past?

My sister, my darling, has passed away—
　　She is not dead, but sleeping;
Again we will meet, in a short earthly day,
　　Then why are we still weeping!
We should gladly rejoice that the pride of our life
Was transplanted above all this war, sin, and
　　strife.

All send kindest greeting from over the sea—
　　Not a word that can wound the full heart;
Full of deep tender feeling and sympathy,
　　Their letters but cheer impart:
Then shall I for this, but a national pride,
Cast the friends of my childhood's days aside?

No, I love the fair South, and my heart would
    bound
  In its fullness of ecstacy,
Could but the glad cry from each hill resound—
    We are free ! we are free ! we are free !
Yet again I send greeting far over the sea,
Each kind letter thence is thrice welcome to me.

1865.

TO DON JUAN BAZ,

EX-GOV. OF MEXICO.

WELCOME, stranger ! glad I greet thee,
    Welcome to our friendly shore ;
Kindred hearts exult to meet thee,
    Rest thyself in peace once more.

Think not I ignore the anguish
    Which must rack thy soul with pain,
As thou dream'st of those who languish,
    Far across the distant main.

No.   I, too, am homeless, weary,
    Fainting in my worldly strife ;
And I know how very dreary
    'Tis to be alone in life.

'Tis in sympathy I greet thee ;
    May my simple words impart
Some ray of light, a ray to cheat thee
    Of sad thoughts that swell thy heart.

Sept. 20th, 1866.

DISAPPOINTMENT.

OH, how can I live in a torture so wild,
　　And yet always be dreaming of bliss ?
Why not learn Fate has doomed me to be sorrow's
　　　　child,
　　And in meekness the heavy rod kiss ?

I have lived for long months in a bright land of
　　　　dreams,
　　Dawning roseate as th' opening of day ;
But alas ! the bright tints were but lightning gleams,
　　Flashing wrath, and then fading away.

True bliss of the soul I have constantly sought,
　　But alas ! I have sought it in vain ;
On earth its base semblance is rended and bought,
　　And I never will seek it again.

How I long for some spot in the solitude deep,
 All alone I could dwell there for years ;
My only companion, Repentance, and weep
 Living fountains of sorrowful tears.

I feel we are drifting too surely apart,
 And sadly I think of the pain,
For my loss, which will gnaw the proud core of
  your heart,
 As alone you sail over life's main.

Oh, why do I sorrow ? I know there is rest
 For the weary, in mansions above ;
And I long to go home to the land of the blest,
 And drink deep of God's pardoning love.

GONE.

"She was beautiful in life
And beautiful in death."

GONE, with all her sparkling beauty,
    Gone, with innocence and youth ;
Gone, with loving ways and kindness,
    Gone, with happiness and truth.

In the tomb they gently laid her—
    Even strangers dropped a tear ;
And one heart will feel the anguish
    Of her loss for many a year.

Father, mother, loving sisters,
    Deeply mourn the lov'd and lost ;
Who can tell the crushing sorrow
    Of the heart who lov'd her most ?

Oft, I fancy, in the twilight,
    That I see her winning face ;
Dream to find, ah, sad awakening !
    I was gazing into space.

Sister, this our earthly parting,
    Will not, cannot, be for aye ;
We will meet, ah, soon, my darling,
    Where there is eternal day !

"I WAS A STRANGER AND YE TOOK ME IN.'

TOSSED on the stormy waves of time,
 By sternest cares oppressed,
I sought and found in Northern clime
 A holy place of rest.

Blessed, thrice blessed be this spot,
 Abiding place of peace,—
May trouble's hand pollute it not,
 And only joys increase.

And you, fair Annie, may your days
 Be fraught with joy and lightness ;
May thornless flowers bestrew your ways,
 And all your hours be brightness.

THE DRUNKARD'S WIFE.

HOW slowly glide the hours by, the minutes
    hours seem ;
Ah ! can such misery be real, or is it but a dream ?
'Tis passing strange that such as this should be
    my lot in life—
The curse I've always dreaded most,—to be an
    unloved wife.

The lark sung blithely as he left, quite early in
    the day ;
The noon-time came, and then the night, and still
    he stays away ;
Alas ! I am too lonely now, for the children are
    asleep,
And I have nothing else to do, but watch, and
    wait, and weep.

The moon is shining brightly, and her calm and
      chilly beams
Would woo me if they could to seek the fairy land
      of dreams ;
And the stars look down with pity from their lofty
      thrones above,
And tell me of the many things I have on earth
      to love.

Ah ! earth is very beautiful : its sunshine and its
      flowers
Can truly heal the broken heart, and cheer its
      lonely hours ;
But, ah ! when night comes—lonely night, with all
      its starry train,—
The new-healed wound, the broken heart, begins to
      bleed again.

How endless seems this dreary night ! and yet,
      'tis only ten ;
I ask aloud, " when will he come ?"   Echo repeats
      the " when ?"

I fancy in each leaf that falls, 'tis his footsteps I hear;
But I will learn to school myself, nor deign to shed
    a tear.

Eleven, now ! the night wears on, and still I am
    alone,—
How favored are the mortals who are blessed with
    hearts of stone !
My Father, on thy daughters look with pitying
    eye, I pray ;
Ere such a lot in life be theirs, take them from
    life away.

Ah ! oft, too oft, such lives of woe merge into lives
    of sin ;
Poor woman's heart must bow before some image
    loved within ;
Man's love must guide her footsteps, and her daily
    pathway cheer—
Then can it be a sin to love the one who holds
    her dear ?

'Tis twelve o'clock !   How can I still this throbbing
    of my brain ?

I wonder how much life like this makes loving
    wives insane !

Each passing sound—the gentle breeze falls on my
    ear like fire,

And yet I dread to hear his voice—I dread the
    drunkard's ire !

The ceaseless ticking of the clock, with hollow,
    vocal sound,

Smites on my heart with boding voice, that leaves
    a bleeding wound :

And now, 'tis on the stroke of one !   Will this
    night never end ?

The watch-dog's bark, the mock-bird's note, and
    cock's shrill clarion blend.

Another hour rolls slowly on, and in the distant west

The pale moon hides her pearly beams, by sinking
    down to rest ;

And now adown the distant road his horse I surely
hear—
Ah, yes ! ah, yes ! his maudlin tones fall on my
listening ear.

"Down, Flora, down! here, Pup, come here !
Why, puppies, are you glad
To see your master home again ? I believe the
dogs are mad !"
And now he comes with tottering steps, and fury
in his eye—
Ah ! if I could, right gladly would I lay me down
and die.

How can I bear this heavy load—for months,
perhaps for years ;
Wear out my life of misery with sorrow, sin, and
tears ?
How long ! how long ! how long ! oh, Lord, will
last this life of strife ?
And shall I always—always be a drunkard's
wretched wife ?

THE FATHER'S LOVE.

FAR more priceless than the diamonds rare
     from Golconda's rich mine ;
Far more precious than the laurel wreaths that
     victor's brows entwine,
Is the garland that fond memory weaves, and
     twines about the heart—
For care nor time, nor war nor crime, can make its
     tints depart.

A mother's love ! most sacred boon to mortals
     ever given ;
'Tis not of earth ; a mother's love was surely born
     in heaven !
See with what gentle, tender care her darling child
     she shields
From harms of life, from every strife this sphere
     terrestrial yields !

But ah, to me, of all the buds in memory's garland
    fair,—
And I have there full many a gem of worth and
    beauty rare,—
Is remembrance of my Father's love, that ever
    shineth bright !
To me, its ray tells of the day that dawns upon
    the night.

He gave to me a double share—a Joseph's sacred
    part,—
And it twined itself, like ivy-green, about my
    infant heart.
I have revelled in gay fashion's throng, have bowed
    at folly's shrine,
But I am sure my heart is pure, while Father's
    love is mine.

All other love is mockery to this, a Father's love—
Fit emblem of the strength of His, who dwelleth
    far above :

More lasting than eternity—more boundless than
  the sea !
The blessing mine, the ray divine, may Father's
  love e'er be.

BURIAL OF A FAIRY QUEEN.

ON a verdant summer islet
  I beheld a wondrous scene,
In a trance of dreamy waking—
  Burial of a Fairy Queen !

First I heard some small pipes playing,
  Like faint night-winds on the breeze,
Or the sound of distant rain-drops,
  As they fall among the trees.

Floating softly o'er the waters,
  And from every bell of foam,
The fairy anthem echoed sweetly,
  Sad as thoughts of distant home.

Next the sound, as if of footsteps,
    O'er the grass plot mov'd along ;
And distinctly came the accents
    Of the solemn funeral song.

Like the melting of the dew-drops,
    Without words of grief or death,
Was the soul-enthralling music,
    Scarcely louder than a breath.

Then my dreaming eyes were opened,
    And in wonder I espied
Thousands of the fairy creatures
    In a circle, side by side.

Scarcely taller than the leaflets
    Of the herbage on the plain,
While their heads were bowed with anguish,
    And their tear-drops fell like rain.

In the middle of the circle,
    On a plat of grass most green,
Stood a bier of unknown flowers,
    Whereon lay the Fairy Queen.

Ah, she was pale as any lily,
    Cold and motionless as snow !
Fainter grew their solemn dirges,
    And still deeper grew their wo !

Two sisters of the queenly fairy,
    Stood at her feet and head,
And sang heart-broken measures,
    Their requiems o'er the dead.

Scarcely louder than the twittering
    Of the wood-lark's dewy breath—
But too full of desolation,
    And the dark despair of death !

Then the flower-bier sank gently,
   At the spot whereon it lay ;
And the magic turf clos'd o'er it—
   Thus the dead queen pass'd away !

Bright dew-drops glittered on the sward—
   One fleet moment more, and then
The mystic troop sailed duskily,
   And far from mortal ken.

The silence of the still midnight
   The murmuring waters broke ;
The moon, emerging from a cloud,
   Shone on me, and I woke.

MYSTERIES OF LIFE.

G OD said, "Let there be light, and there was
  light,"
Created from the darkness infinite :
And from the waters, called he forth the Earth,
And Heaven rejoiced at this, her sister's birth.
The Earth brought forth the grass, the herb, the
  tree,
And flowers, bright flowers, so priceless and so
  free.
The heavens, God decked with mighty gems of
  light,
Sol ruled the day, the moon and stars the night.
" Let waters bring forth creatures that have life."
On earth, in air, in water there was strife.

God saw that all his wondrous work was good,
As on his throne of Holiness he stood.
One thing was wanting, and the world so fair,
He perfect made ; He placed his image there.
And woman too—of man the better part,
He made to twine herself about man's heart.
We gaze upon all natural works sublime,
Mark daily births, and sad decay of time :
We see flowers blooming—see them fade away—
We see bright visions vanish in a day :
We dream of joy—of perfect earthly bliss,
Dreams soft and sweet, yet fleeting as a kiss.
The wild wind comes—ah, whither does it go ?
From whence do all these gushing waters flow ?
Why do the roots take moisture from the soil ?
And beauteous flowers neither spin nor toil ;
Yet they in robes of splendor are arrayed,
Of texture fine, and colors of each shade.
Birds, beasts, and flowers, throughout our beau-
        teous land,
Mysterious works of an Almighty hand.

In vain we seek solution here to find,
Of these great problems—earth and all mankind.
Man is the greatest mystery of life,
For in his soul are passions ever rife.
He in his Saviour's mighty image plann'd,
To love, to hate, to serve, and to command:
Yet changing ever—one thing but a day;
First young, then old, then passing quite away.
In his blind ignorance doomed to never know,
From whence he cometh, whither he will go.
Perchance his soul once lived in a bright flower,
Which bloomed and faded in a short sweet hour;
Perchance he dwelt in yonder twinkling stars—
In loving Venus, or the warlike Mars;
In youth he ever craves to be of age,
In age he sighs while reading memory's page
Forever filled with longings undefined,
With high-wrought fancies of a craving mind:
Craving, alas! but doomed to never find
Congenial nature to our hearts to bind.

Yearning for something cloudy as a dream,
He grasps the rainbow, finds it lightning's gleam.

The soul drinks beauty from each hill and dale,
The clouds of sunset and the flowery vale ;

Revels amid the histories of yore,
Drinks deep of knowledge, wildly craves for more.

He is ambitious—he seeks lasting fame,
Will earth defy to win immortal name.

He would be happy.   Ah, all joy, all bliss
Lasts but a moment in a world like this.

Why should we seek to solve this mystery ?
Through time 'twill last, until Eternity ;

We know that God, in his omnipotence,
Will make dark, light, when we are called from
        hence.

And then alone, when ceases this frail breath,
We'll read the mystery of Life, and Death.

LINES UPON THE DEATH OF

CHARLEY DU BIGNON.

THE years of manhood had not tinged
    His young life with their gloom,
He tasted not the bitter cup
    That comes with life's full bloom,

Of fond hopes wrecked, ambition crushed,
    'Till doubting even truth,
The sternest soul would hide itself
    In memories of youth.

He saw not that in friendship's smile,
    Was lurking hate, deceit ;
Nor had he proven earthly bliss,
    A mirage, dream—a cheat.

While youth sees but the beautiful,
    The sunshine and the flowers,
Maturity will have its cares,
    And winter its cold showers.

Fortune bestowed on this her child,
    High heritage, proud birth,—
Dame Nature added, as her dower,
    Rare gifts of untold worth ;

More priceless than most sparkling gems,
    As pure as gold refined ;
Most glorious birth-right—sacred gifts,
    A noble heart and mind.

How his proud, young soul revolted
    At oppression's cruel reign,
And he rushed forth to the battle-field,
    Our freedom to regain.

He thought not of his slender frame,
    His heart was filled with might ;
His armor God—Truth for his shield—
    His watchwords, Freedom ! Right !

Alas, alas ! where are they now,
    Our noble, good—our braves ?
Does our shame reflect upon them ?
    No, they rest in soldiers' graves.

And the old star-spangled banner,
    Dyed with gore above us waves,
And our gallant dead are freemen,
    And the living Union's slaves.

Then mourn not, parents, for your son,
    Your much-beloved—your pride ;
He dwells above this earthly sphere,
    Where lasting joys abide.

When this troubled dream is over,
　　You will meet your boy again ,
Ah, you would not then recall him
　　To this earth of war and pain ?

Then mourn not, parents, for your dead,
　　But think that his pure name
Is on the list with those who wear
　　The laurel wreath of fame.

WE MET.

WE met, and memory flew to joys and tears,
　　Back through the vista dim, of long-past
years.
In my childhood's home I was a child again—
A home to me, save only in the name.

And yet I loved it, for there grew apace
Four lovely children ripening into grace ;
If 'twas not home, they sisters were to me,
And even now their fairy forms I see.

Once by a tomb, alone I stood so drear—
Dropped on a mother's grave a daughter's tear.
A soft voice murmured, " She's my mother too ;
Sister, I'll put some flowers there for you."

God bless the child, she was too fair for earth ;
Such flowers as she should have immortal birth ;
And so God took our darling home on high,
Where she will bloom to never fade and die.

No stranger was she in that home above,
Where she was greeted with a mother's love ;
A wife stood waiting for a husband's child ;
A sister welcomed with a gladness mild.

We met, and I to him brought back—not years,
But months deep fraught, alas, with joys and tears.
That child a maiden grown, stood by his side ;
His light, his life, his darling, promised bride.

Again he stood by that sad bed of death,
And felt the painful throbbing of her breath.
" I am so weary that I fain would rest—
Oh, darling, place my head upon your breast."

We meet with hearts fast bound by mutual grief ;
We knew that sympathy could give relief ;
So when our stranger hands were joined together,
A lonely sister found a loving brother.

DRINK ON.

TAKE in hand the cup of delusion,
    With your eyes on the future, drink ;
Scorn the results, however appalling,
        Tho' you see that you stand upon Hell's
        dark brink.

The bubbles that float on the top of the cup
    Are only the tears of your wife !
You have drained her happiness in the draught—
    Drink on, you will drain her life.

Drink on, fill the glowing cup anew—
    Now the drops look red, blood red :
It is only the blood of your little ones—
    And their doom rests on your head !

Drink then, drink on ; take the cup to your lips !
   What matter if parents' grey hairs
Are floating upon its surface in scores !
   Drink on, you will drown your cares !

Drink then, drink on ; for you must take the
       cup—
   'Tis no longer a matter of will ;
No longer the cup of habit or choice—
   But the cup of punishment—fill !

Yes, drain the cup to the bitter dregs,
   While the fiends laugh at your pains ;
And exult to know that but wretchedness
   In the tempting wine remains.

SPEAK TO HER TENDERLY.

SPEAK to her tenderly, taunt her not now,
   Tho' a million of sins hath deep furrowed
      her brow;
Greet her with kindness.   Her once raven hair
Is frosted with silver time's hand hath left there.

Cheeks now so colorless, bloomed like the rose;
Lips now all tremulous, spoke but repose;
Dim eyes, all clouded with fountains of tears,
Were like the young fawn's eyes, in long agone
      years.

Speak to her tenderly.   How can you know
Why bowed her young soul 'neath temptation's
      fell blow?

It may be that poverty planted the seed—
Tears nourished its growth, Pride matured the
rank weed.

It may be, she loved, tho' unwisely, too well;
It may be, the serpent allured, with his spell,
That from his sweet charming she woke but to
know
The death in life sorrow—the *all-alone woe.*

It may be, in sinning, she erred but to save
A dear one from filling want's desolate grave;
Perchance some unkindness first drove to despair,
A manly heart saved her, she wept her grief there.

Then judge not too harshly. Remorse's heavy
hand
Is a terrible stricture—an icy-cold band;
Long years of repentance, of praying, and pain,
And the blood of the Saviour, hath cleansed her
from stain !

KNITTING.

MY muse is in the sulks to-day,
　　I've tried in vain to find
A subject fit for rhyme and song,
　　Just suited to my mind.

I called last night upon the stars,
　　To-day upon the sun,—
My muse would leave me in the lurch,
　　With just a line begun.

I tried to work, I tried to sing,
　　And then I tried to play ;
And then I took my knitting up,
　　To while the time away.

And then the flashes of quick thought,
    With bliss thrilled all my soul ;
With every stitch did fancy's hand,
    A saddening page unroll.

The dullest of the dullest work,
    So tiresome, and so slow !
To knit, and knit, the live-long day,
    And still small increase show

But as I knit, a fairy web
    My brain wore in its dreaming,
And in each stitch my fancy saw
    Some bright poetic gleaming.

And stitch by stitch the work goes on,
    For some proud soldier brave,
Who may, perchance, these stitches wear,
    Into a soldier's grave.

Far away from mother, sister—
 Aye, from wife and daughter true,
With their feet all bare and bleeding,
 And their hearts all bleeding too.

Now, perchance, one may be lying
 Wounded on the cold earth damp,
While so feebly, faintly burning,
 Is the last light of life's lamp.

Bright visions of the happy past,
 Move slow before his eyes—
And then the mocking present comes
 To taunt him ere he dies.

The glorious future once so bright,
 To him has now grown dim—
Alone he dies, while song-birds sing
 The solemn funeral hymn.

Ah ! in some distant cottage,
    His dear wife knitting there,
Is sending with each stitch she takes,
    An earnest, heartfelt prayer.

She little thinks, as, in her pride,
    She rolls the finished pair,
That his loved feet are cold and still,
    And his body free from care.

God grant that in the future,
    The bliss may be in store,
That they may meet in heaven above—
    Aye, meet to part no more.

Fond mother, cease your knitting,
    For your boy with curly hair
Is dead upon the battle-field,
    So cold, and, oh, so fair !

Poor child, why did they send him—
　　Too young, and yet so brave,
To be a bullet's shining mark,
　　And fill a soldier's grave?

Bend gently o'er him, comrades—
　　Drop on his curls a tear—
Write on his rude-carved head board,
　　A mother's pride sleeps here.

A mother's joy—her treasure,
　　A widow's only son,
Has gained the life eternal.—
　　Death's victory is won.

Around his noble brow is twined
　　The laurel wreath of fame,—
The mother's darling boy has now
　　A never-dying name.

I will not say, I will not think,
    Knitting is dull, again ;
For, from steel needles sparkling thoughts
    Will fly into the brain.

LINES ON THE DEATH OF THE

REV. S. K. TALMAGE.

MOURN not, friends, mourn not, bereaved,
  That his earthly race is run ;
He hath reached the gates celestial,
  Over death the victory won.

Moulded in his Father's image,
  He the Saviour's footsteps trod ;
And God claimed his sainted spirit,
  Ere the body reached the sod.

Ah ! ye would not then recall him,
  But a tenement of clay ;
Bless, oh ! bless God, that his mercy,
  Called his loved one away.

Meek and lowly, pure in spirit—
    Humble as a little child—
Mighty in his love of Jesus—
    He is with the undefiled.

Ever ready with his counsel,
    And his prayers to guide the young ;
Choirs of redeemed sinners,
    When he died, the requiem sung.

Mourn not, friends, mourn not, bereaved,
    That his earthly race is run ;
He hath reached the goal eternal,
    Over death the victory won.

TO ANNIE.

ANNIE, my first-born, gentle child,
    My tender, fragile flower ;
Why twines thy image round my heart,
    With such mysterious power ?

Is it because thy infant wail
    The icy barrier moved,
That bound my soul's affections fast ?
    I knew 'twas mine I loved.

A mother's love no tongue can tell—
    How boundless is that sea !
'Twas never mine ; her spirit fled,
    As she gave birth to me.

Annie, I gave to thee, my child,
   The love my heart could yield ;
God grant its influence o'er thee cast
   From all life's ills a shield.

THE BEAUTIFUL.

THE beautiful ! what is not perfect here below,
 Created by the great Almighty power ?
Each grain of sand Omnipotence doth show,
 And beauty beameth in the humblest flower.

There's beauty in the budding leaves of spring,
 In the maturity of summer born—
And in the many hues that autumn's bring,
 And in bright winter's glittering sheen at dawn.

Mark you the smallest insect's many hues ;
 What beauty in their ever changing shade !
The diamond glistening of the morning dews,—
 The sunbeams on the ocean's bosom stayed.

Night robed in darkness, and with bright gems
      crowned ;
  The silvery softness of the midnight moon ;
The sunrise-sky, with gold and blue zone-bound ;
    The fiery splendor of the day at noon.

The snow-white summit of the mountain proud ;
    The solemn stillness of the flowery dell ;
The fleecy brightness of the sun-capped cloud ;
    The gem-decked chambers of the ocean's cell.

There's regal grandeur in the rushing storm ;
    There's sweetness in the gentle rain soft falling ;
There's splendor in the lightning's dazzling form,
    And thunder is majestic, yet appalling.

See life and beauty in the thoughtless child—
    The nobler beauty of good manhood's grace ;
The saintlier beauty of the aged mild,
    Who waiteth summons to the resting place.

Can ye not see the beautiful repose,
    O'er all the earth ?   How blind then, are your
        eyes !
For there is dearth of beauty but to those
    Who scorn the Giver, and His gifts despise.

THE BEAUTIFUL SEA.

I HAVE pined for the sight of the sea for years—
   Pined amid hoping, and wished amid fears ;
And my heart grew glad, and it bounded in glee
At the sight of the broad expanse of the sea.

The sea, the beautiful, beautiful sea—
Beautiful, boundless, joyful and free !
See how they glimmer, those white-capped waves,
Reflecting the sunlight from deep ocean caves !
Can things so bright and beautiful, hide
The breakers that rise and sink with the tide ?

There, see that gay gleaming of white, bead-like
      spray,
Transformed to a rainbow by Sol's colors gay ;
It gleams for a moment, and then disappears,
Like lost pleasures, as seen through despair's briny
      tears.

Far, far in the distance, the houses so white,
Faintly show through their veiling of green, red
　　　　and light ;
Very soon the dry land we shall leave far away,
And onward we'll bound o'er the billows so gay.

But what is the matter ? what is the little swell ?
It can surely be nothing—I still feel quite well ;
Then another, another, another small swell,
And my feelings are too undefined now to tell—
And the sea at length loses its silvery light,
And its snow-capped, bright waves grow as dark as
　　　　midnight.

Ah, what has become of those laughing young
　　　　graces
Who entered the vessel with bright, smiling faces ?
Their gladness is lost in the swell of the sea,
And to Neptune they pray from their ills to be free.
I laugh, I can't help it, to see the distress ;
And yet—I am sick myself, nevertheless !

'Tis the vessel that tosses, she sinks and she heaves,
And my sea-admiration all quits me and leaves.
I am sick as the mischief !   The sea, oh, the sea !
Thou hast lost all thy charms and thy beauty to me.

Sick ? is there no word in our language to tell
The nausea and anguish of that rolling and swell ?
'Tis so funny to see how each quick, sudden lurch,
Brings down a new victim from Romance's perch.

And now comes that torment—that Tom—the
      young sinner !
Says he, " darling sister, shall I bring up your
      dinner ?"
Bah ! dinner, you torment ! oh, pray drown me,
      quick,
For I am so miserable—sick, oh, so sick !
The men, how I hate them ! just see how they
      smile
At our torture, because they are well all the while.

Such pitching and tossing—inexpressible woe !
For we heave with the vessel, and join in each
      throe ;
The faces around me I cannot portray—
But they show their disgust of the billows so gay.

There is nothing, no, nothing, can bring us relief
From this torture of tortures, this grief of all grief.
The sea, the boundless expanse of the sea,
Thrills others with rapture, but cannot charm me.

HUGGING THE SHORE.

"DO you think you will hug the shore,
      Captain, to-day?"
Asked a saucy young flirt, with a smile ;
    With crimson flush was dyed her cheek,
And over her brow swept the roseate hue,
While her eyes revealed in their dancing blue
    All the lips declined to speak.

The captain glanced at the distant shore,
    And then at the maid awhile—
The shore was distant, and she was near,
And the rose-tint deepened, as he said, "Dear,
    I'll neglect the shore to-day!"

And around her waist crept the captain's hand—
It was so much better than hugging dry land !
And he said, glancing over the vessel's bow,
" The ship is hugging Cape Hatteras now,
　　But I'll hug the Cape of May."

CHRISTMAS, SOUTH, 1866.

LAUGHING, merry, childish voices, woke us
      in their eager glee,
When the rosy blush of morning in the east we
      scarce could see :
Surely, ne'er a Christmas morning was so cold and
      drear as this ;
Can it be our hearts are frozen with the sere frost's
      icy kiss ?
Ah, stern want and desolation has a heavy, heavy
      hand,
And no mirth should ever issue from beneath the
      iron band.
Now the voices draw still nearer—bless the
      children, all are here !
"Mother, don't weep, they won't mind it ; oh,
      God help thee, mother, dear !"

One by one they took their stockings, gazed upon
    the store, then turned :

" Sissic," said the bravest rebel, " did Santee have
    his cotton burned ?"

" Hush, hush, Buddie ; don't say nothing ; just see
    how poor mamma cries."

Now the repentant Buddy to his mother's bedside
    hies—

" I'm so sorry, mother, darling : when I'm grown
    you shan't be poor ;

I'll write for the Yankee papers, that will make us
    rich once more."

Off I turned to hide my feelings—feelings deep by
    care refined,—

Ah ! my child, like sister Annie's, your poor piece
    may be declined.

Ah, there is some joy in sorrow ! in the door two
    freed-men creep :

" Christmas gif, ole Mis, Miss Annie—why, what
    fur you white folks weep ?

All dis time you give us Christmas ; now, we going
    to give to you :

Here, old Missus, here, Miss Annie—children, here's
    your Christmas, too !"

In black bosoms true love lingers, deeply by our
    kindness riven,

And the tender tie that binds us, can be severed
    save by heaven.

O'er the day that dawned so sadly, that kind act
    a ray imparts,

And we grasp the sunbeam gladly, for it cheers
    our aching hearts.

A LOVE-LETTER.

YOU wished for a love-letter, Doctor—but
    then,
I know you to be most conceited of men ;
You'll think I'm in earnest, I vow now I ain't,
For I would not deign to love even a saint.

You must never believe what the fair ladies say:
Take their nay for a yes, and their yes for a nay.
Like doctors, the darlings are very deceiving,
And most that they say is not half worth believing.

But now for my letter.   How shall I begin ?
If I say, my dear Doctor, that will be a sin !
And a love-letter without dear, darling, or dove,
Would be as insipid as one without love.

Love, glorious love, with its grand mystic art,
Sways each mortal mind, and scathes each human
   heart ;
Without care or regret it inflicts pain or joy,
Tossing high the frail heart that becomes its day's
   toy.

It drinks up the life-sap, becomes life itself,
Regardless of true love, of beauty or pelf—
An object most " homely " in love's eye I ween—
Will seem like an angel, as bright as a queen.

It glosses its object, like man's serpent tongue—
Makes even the aged appear as if young ;
Waving locks to love's eye, e'en if sprinkled with
   gray,
Does not lessen, but strengthens its powerful sway.

Love, bright, joyous love, heals each sad, breaking
   heart,
But breaks it again when it strives to depart :

For the void, when once filled by love, never again
A vision can fill it, save only great pain.

The blessing of blessings, the greatest of woes,
Will leave its bright signet wherever it goes :
Then seek love and find it, whenever you can—
My counsel is needless, for you are a—man.

Now, Doctor, I'm sure that this letter you'll find
Is suited exactly to your turn of mind ;
I've sent what I promised—a true loving letter,—
And if it don't suit you, why, just write a better !

TO ONE WHO SLEEPETH.

WRITTEN BY A SCHOOL-HOUSE WELL.

LONG years have passed since first a merry
child,
I quaffed the precious drink with eager joy,
And dashed the silvery drops, with laughter wild,
Upon the saucy youth, and maiden coy.

To the old well we wandered, hand in hand,
And by the way we cull'd each new-blown flower;
Then near the large old oak-tree we would stand,
And fashion wreaths to wither in an hour.

With a large leaf you made a tiny cup,
And call'd me then your little fairy queen;
And you, the king, would dip the water up—
Most faithful subject in my realm, I ween.

Up to the sky we built a mighty pile
    Of lofty, splendid castles in the air ;
Then dashed them down, you laughing all the while
    At my half-smiling and half-sad despair.

We watched the others as they came to drink
    With lore prophetic did their fortunes tell ;
All by the way they made the bucket sink,
    With motion fast or slow, down in the well.

How often shelter'd from the sudden shower,
    Beneath the roof we'd sit, and sweetly dream ;
Charmed with the lightning's swift and dazzling
            power,
    We reached our hands to grasp the fatal gleam.

Then when the sun its radiant beams did lend
    The glorious beauty of the clouds t' unfold.
We sought in vain to reach the rainbow's end—
    To find a treasure there—a pot of gold !

Too short, alas ! would be our dream of bliss—
    For wakened by the school-bell's lively ring,
We did, as mortals must, in earth like this,
    Our airy thoughts to things terrestrial bring.

Long years have passed, and once again I stand
    Upon the brink of this much-loved old well ;
An alien and a stranger in the land,
    Drawn thither by some mystic charm or spell.

Where are ye now, friends of my early days ?
    Why stand I here so desolate and lone ?
Alas ! alas ! all gone their earthly ways,
    Or in the angel throngs around God's throne.

And you who swore to win, in youthful pride,
    The laurel wreath of fame to deck your brow,
And then to come and claim me as your bride—
    Where are you now ? oh, God ! where are you
        now ?

Oh, that your sainted spirit had the power
　　To seek the earth, and on this loved spot stand,
That I could tell you, in this twilight hour,
　　All my past life, while clasping hand in hand :

Could put my hand upon your manly breast,
　　And tell you since the night, to young love's
　　　dawn,
The saddening shadows of a life unblest,
　　Veil-like athwart my spirit have been drawn.

And tell you, ere the flush of youth was past,
　　All bright hopes faded from my sight away ;
And how I wished each hour could be my last,
　　For to me, time was night without its day.

How sadly I have roved from shore to shore—
　　Sought happiness in palace and in cot :
And still I seek, and shall forever more.—
　　But shall I find it ?　Ah, you answer not !

How I have quaffed from pleasure's giddy cup,
    And sought to win a never-dying name !
Alas ! to taste with but the smallest sup
    The bitter that is mixed with sweets of fame.

I am not wretched now.   The heavy cloud
    That shaded from my sight each joyous gleam,
And robed my spirit, as if with a shroud,
    Has passed away. I see the moon's pale beam :

Peace should content me, but we mortals crave
    Some earthly fame, some happiness and love ;
But disappointed soon we reach the grave,
    And find such bliss alone in heaven above.

In heaven ?   Oh, tell me from that other shore,
    Where with the favored beings of God you
        dwell—
Is there a place they torture evermore—
    Oh, is there without doubt a heaven or hell ?

Say, will the doors of heaven be open thrown
    To all who sorrow for a life of sin,
Far upward by their strong repentance borne—
    Say, can such stricken, weary souls go in ?

Why do I doubt ! I know there is a heaven,
    And that this life is nothing but a dream,
And hope one day, with all my sins forgiven,
    To meet thee where all things are what they
        seem !

I must away, for now the night draws nigh,
    And stars begin to glimmer o'er my head :
Ah ! would my home was up above the sky—
    My name, with yours, was numbered with the
        dead.

INFELICIA.

Monday first october 1867

Dear Miss Menken

I shall have great pleasure
in accepting your dedication, and
I thank you for your portrait as a
highly remarkable specimen of
Photography.

I also thank you for the verses
enclosed in your note. Many such
welcomes come to me, but few so
pathetically written, and fewer still
so modestly sent.—

Faithfully Yours

Charles Dickens

INFELICIA.

ADAH ISAACS MENKEN.

PHILADELPHIA:

J. B. LIPPINCOTT & CO.

INFELICIA

BY

ADAH ISAACS MENKEN.

———

PHILADELPHIA:
J. B. LIPPINCOTT & CO.
1873.

Leaves pallid and sombre and ruddy
  Dead fruits of the fugitive years;
Some stained as with wine and made bloody,
  And some as with tears."

CONTENTS.

INFELICIA.

RESURGAM.

I.

YES, yes, dear love ! I am dead !
   Dead to you !
   Dead to the world !
   Dead for ever !
It was one young night in May.
The stars were strangled, and the moon was blind with the
      flying clouds of a black despair.

Years and years the songless soul waited to drift out
beyond the sea of pain where the shapeless life was
wrecked.

The red mouth closed down the breath that was hard
and fierce.

The mad pulse beat back the baffled life with a low
sob.

And so the stark and naked soul unfolded its wings to
the dimness of Death !

A lonely, unknown Death.

A Death that left this dumb, living body as his endless
mark.

And left these golden billows of hair to drown the whiteness of my bosom.

Left these crimson roses gleaming on my forehead to hide the dust of the grave.

And Death left an old light in my eyes, and old music for my tongue, to deceive the crawling worms that would seek my warm flesh.

But the purple wine that I quaff sends no thrill of Love and Song through my empty veins.

Yet my red lips are not pallid and horrified.

Thy kisses are doubtless sweet that throb out an eternal passion for me !

But I feel neither pleasure, passion nor pain.

So I am certainly dead.

Dead in this beauty !

Dead in this velvet and lace !

Dead in these jewels of light !

Dead in the music !

Dead in the dance !

II.

Why did I die ?

O love ! I waited—I waited years and years ago.

Once the blaze of a far-off edge of living Love crept up my horizon and promised a new moon of Poesy.

A soul's full life !

A soul's full love !

And promised that my voice should ring trancing shivers of rapt melody down the grooves of this dumb earth.

And promised that echoes should vibrate along the pu

ple spheres of unfathomable seas, to the soundless folds of the clouds.

And promised that I should know the sweet sisterhood of the stars.

Promised that I should live with the crooked moon in her eternal beauty.

But a Midnight swooped down to bridegroom the Day.

The blazing Sphynx of that far off, echoless promise, shrank into a drowsy shroud that mocked the crying stars of my soul's unuttered song.

And so I died.

Died this uncoffined and unburied Death.

Died alone in the young May night.

Died with my fingers grasping the white throat of many a prayer.

III.

Yes, dear love, I died!

You smile because you see no cold, damp cerements of a lonely grave hiding the youth of my fair face.

No head-stone marks the gold of my poor unburied head.

But the flaunting poppy covered her red heart in the sand.

Who can hear the slow drip of blood from a dead soul?

No Christ of the Past writes on my laughing brow His "Resurgam."

Resurgam.

What is that when I have been dead these long weary years!

IV.

Silver walls of Sea !

Gold and spice laden barges !

White-sailed ships from Indian seas, with costly pearls and tropic wines go by unheeding !

None pause to lay one token at my feet.

No mariner lifts his silken banner for my answering hail.

No messages from the living to the dead.

Must all lips fall out of sound as the soul dies to be heard ?

Shall Love send back no revelation through this interminable distance of Death ?

Can He who promised the ripe Harvest forget the weeping Sower ?

How can I stand here so calm ?

I hear the clods closing down my coffin, and yet shriek not out like the pitiless wind, nor reach my wild arms after my dead soul !

Will no sun of fire again rise over the solemn East ?

I am tired of the foolish moon showing only her haggard face above the rocks and chasms of my grave.

O Rocks ! O Chasms ! sink back to your black cradles in the West !

Leave me dead in the depths !

Leave me dead in the wine !

Leave me dead in the dance !

V.

How did I die ?

The man I loved—he—he—ah, well !

There is no voice from the grave.

The ship that went down at sea, with seven times a thousand souls for Death, sent back no answer.

The breeze is voiceless that saw the sails shattered in the mad tempest, and heard the cry for mercy as one frail arm clung to the last spar of the sinking wreck.

Fainting souls rung out their unuttered messages to the silent clouds.

Alas! I died not so!

I died not so!

VI.

How did I die?

No man has wrenched his shroud from his stiffened corpse to say:

"*Ye murdered me!*"

No woman has died with enough of Christ in her soul to tear the bandage from her glassy eyes and say:

"*Ye crucified me!*"

Resurgam! Resurgam!

DREAMS OF BEAUTY.

VISIONS of Beauty, of Light, and of Love,
   Born in the soul of a Dream,
Lost, like the phantom-bird under the dove,
   When she flies over a stream—

Come ye through portals where angel wings droop,
   Moved by the heaven of sleep?
Or, are ye mockeries, crazing a soul,
   Doomed with its waking to weep?

I could believe ye were shadows of earth,
   Echoes of hopes that are vain,
But for the music ye bring to my heart,
   Waking its sunshine again.

And ye are fleeting.   All vainly I strive
   Beauties like thine to portray;
Forth from my pencil the bright picture starts,
   And—ye have faded away.

Like to a bird that soars up from the spray,
   When we would fetter its wing;
Like to the song that spurns Memory's grasp
   When the voice yearneth to sing;

14

Like the cloud-glory that sunset lights up,
　　When the storm bursts from its height;
Like the sheet-silver that rolls on the sea,
　　When it is touched by the night—

Bright, evanescent, ye come and are gone,
　　Visions of mystical birth;
Art that could paint you was never vouchsafed
　　Unto the children of earth.

Yet in my soul there's a longing to tell
　　All you have seemed unto me,
That unto others a glimpse of the skies
　　You in their sorrow might be.

Vain is the wish.　Better hope to describe
　　All that the spirit desires,
When through a cloud of vague fancies and schemes
　　Flash the Promethean fires.

Let me then think of ye, Visions of Light,
　　Not as the tissue of dreams,
But as realities destined to be
　　Bright in Futurity's beams.

Ideals formed by a standard of earth
　　Sink at Reality's shrine
Into the human and weak like ourselves,
　　Losing the essence divine;

But the fair pictures that fall from above
　　On the heart's mirror sublime

Carry a signature written in tints,
   Bright with the future of time.

And the heart, catching them, yieldeth a spark
   Under each stroke of the rod—
Sparks that fly upward and light the New Life,
   Burning an incense to God!

MY HERITAGE.

"MY heritage!" It is to live within
      The marts of Pleasure and of Gain, yet be
No willing worshiper at either shrine;
To think, and speak, and act, not for my pleasure,
But others'. The veriest slave of time
And circumstances. Fortune's toy!
To hear of fraud, injustice, and oppression,
And feel who is the unshielded victim.
        Cold friends and causeless foes!
        Proud thoughts that rise to fall.
Bright stars that set in seas of blood;
Affections, which are passions, lava-like
Destroying what they rest upon. Love's
Fond and fervid tide preparing icebergs
That fragile bark, this loving human heart.
        O'ermastering Pride!
        Ruler of the Soul!
Life, with all its changes, cannot bow ye.
        Soul-subduing Poverty!
That lays his iron, cold grasp upon the high
Free spirit: strength, sorrow-born, that bends
But breaks not in his clasp—all, all
These are "my heritage!"
And mine to know a reckless human love, all passion

and intensity, and see a mist come o'er the scene, a dimness steal o'er the soul!

Mine to dream of joy and wake to wretchedness!
Mine to stand on the brink of life
One little moment where the fresh'ning breeze
Steals o'er the languid lip and brow, telling
Of forest leaf, and ocean wave, and happy
Homes, and cheerful toil; and bringing gently
To this wearied heart its long-forgotten
Dreams of gladness.

But turning the fevered cheek to meet the soft kiss of the winds, my eyes look to the sky, where I send up my soul in thanks. The sky is clouded—no stars—no music —the heavens are hushed.

My poor soul comes back to me, weary and disappointed.

The very breath of heaven, that comes to all, comes not to me.

Bound in iron gyves of unremitting toil, my vital air is wretchedness—what need I any other?

"My heritage!" The shrouded eye, the trampled leaf, wind-driven and soiled with dust—these tell the tale.

Mine to watch
The glorious light of intellect
Burn dimly, and expire; and mark the soul,
Though born in Heaven, pause in its high career,
Wave in its course, and fall to grovel in
The darkness of earth's contamination, till
Even Death shall scorn to give a thing
So low his welcome greeting!
Who would be that pale,

Blue mist, that hangs so low in air, like Hope
That has abandoned earth, yet reacheth
Not the stars in their proud homes?
A dying eagle, striving to reach the sun?
A little child talking to the gay clouds as they flaunt
past in their purple and crimson robes?
A timid little flower singing to the grand old trees?
Foolish waves, leaping up and trying to kiss the moon?
A little bird mocking the stars?
Yet this is what men call Genius.

JUDITH.

"Repent, or I will come unto thee quickly, and will fight thee with the sword of my mouth."—REVELATION ii. 16.

I.

ASHKELON is not cut off with the remnant of a valley.
  Baldness dwells not upon Gaza.
  The field of the valley is mine, and it is clothed in verdure.
  The steepness of Baal-perazim is mine;
  And the Philistines spread themselves in the valley of Rephaim.
  They shall yet be delivered into my hands.
  For the God of Battles has gone before me!
  The sword of the mouth shall smite them to dust.
  I have slept in the darkness—
  But the seventh angel woke me, and giving me a sword of flame, points to the blood-ribbed cloud, that lifts his reeking head above the mountain.
  Thus am I the prophet.
  I see the dawn that heralds to my waiting soul the advent of power.

Power that will unseal the thunders!
Power that will give voice to graves!

20

Graves of the living ;
Graves of the dying ;
Graves of the sinning ;
Graves of the loving ;
Graves of despairing ;
And oh ! graves of the deserted !
These shall speak, each as their voices shall be loosed.
And the day is dawning.

II.

Stand back, ye Philistines !
Practice what ye preach to me ;
I heed ye not, for I know ye all.
Ye are living burning lies, and profanation to the gar-
ments which with stately steps ye sweep your marble
palaces.
Your palaces of Sin, around which the damning evi-
dence of guilt hangs like a reeking vapor.
Stand back !
I would pass up the golden road of the world.
A place in the ranks awaits me.
I know that ye are hedged on the borders of my path.
Lie and tremble, for ye well know that I hold with iron
grasp the battle axe.
Creep back to your dark tents in the valley.
Slouch back to your haunts of crime.
Ye do not know me, neither do ye see me.
But the sword of the mouth is unsealed, and ye coil
yourselves in slime and bitterness at my feet.
I mix your jeweled heads, and your gleaming eyes, and
your hissing tongues with the dust.

My garments shall bear no mark of ye.

When I shall return this sword to the angel, your foul blood will not stain its edge.

It will glimmer with the light of truth, and the strong arm shall rest.

III.

Stand back !

I am no Magdalene waiting to kiss the hem of your garment.

It is mid-day.

See ye not what is written on my forehead ?

I am Judith !

I wait for the head of my Holofernes !

Ere the last tremble of the conscious death-agony shall have shuddered, I will show it to ye with the long black hair clinging to the glazed eyes, and the great mouth opened in search of voice, and the strong throat all hot and reeking with blood, that will thrill me with wild unspeakable joy as it courses down my bare body and dabbles my cold feet !

My sensuous soul will quake with the burden of so much bliss.

Oh, what wild passionate kisses will I draw up from that bleeding mouth !

I will strangle this pallid throat of mine on the sweet blood !

I will revel in my passion.

At midnight I will feast on it in the darkness.

For it was that which thrilled its crimson tides of reckless passion through the blue veins of my life, and made them leap up in the wild sweetness of Love and agony of Revenge !

I am starving for this feast.

Oh forget not that I am Judith !

And I know where sleeps Holofernes.

WORKING AND WAITING.

Suggested by Carl Müller's Cast of the Seamstress, at the Dusseldorf
Gallery.

I.

LOOK on that form, once fit for the sculptor !
  Look on that cheek, where the roses have died !
Working and waiting have robbed from the artist
  All that his marble could show for its pride.
        Statue-like sitting
        Alone, in the flitting
And wind-haunted shadows that people her hearth.
        God protect all of us—
        God shelter all of us
From the reproach of such scenes upon earth !

II.

All the day long, and through the cold midnight,
  Still the hot needle she wearily plies.
Haggard and white as the ghost of a Spurned One,
  Sewing white robes for the Chosen One's eyes—
        Lost in her sorrow,
        But for the morrow
Phantom-like speaking in every stitch—
        God protect all of us—
        God shelter all of us
From the Curse, born with each sigh for the Rich !

24

III.

Low burns the lamp.   Fly swifter, thou needle—
  Swifter, thou asp for the breast of the poor !
Else the pale light will be stolen by Pity,
  Ere of the vital part thou hast made sure.
      Dying, yet living :
      All the world's giving
Barely the life that runs out with her thread.
      God protect all of us—
      God shelter all of us
From her last glance, as she follows the Dead !

IV.

What if the morning finds her still bearing
  All the soul's load of a merciless lot !
Fate will not lighten a grain of the burden
  While the poor bearer by man is forgot.
      Sewing and sighing !
      Sewing and dying !
What to such life is a day or two more ?
      God protect all of us—
      God shelter all of us
From the new day's lease of woe to the Poor !

V.

Hasten, ye winds ! and yield her the mercy
  Lying in sleep on your purified breath ;
Yield her the mercy, enfolding a blessing,
  Yield her the mercy whose signet is Death.

In her toil stopping,
See her work dropping—
Fate, thou art merciful !   Life, thou art done !
God protect all of us—
God shelter all of us
From the heart breaking, and yet living on !

VI.

Winds that have sainted her, tell ye the story
   Of the young life by the needle that bled ;
Making its bridge over Death's soundless waters
   Out of a swaying and soul-cutting thread.
Over it going,
All the world knowing !
Thousands have trod it, foot-bleeding, before !
God protect all of us—
God shelter all of us,
Should she look back from the Opposite Shore !

THE RELEASE.

I.

"Carry me out of the host, for I am wounded."

THE battle waged strong.

A fainting soul was borne from the host.

The tears robed themselves in the scarlet of guilt, and crowned with iron of wrong, they trod heavily on the wounded soul,

Bound close to the dark prison-walls, with the clanking chains of old Error.

Malice and Envy crept up the slimy sides of the turrets to mark out with gore-stained fingers the slow hours of the night.

The remorseless Past stood ever near, breathing through the broken chords of life its never-ending dirge.

Yet, Ahab-like, the poor soul lingered on, bleeding and pining, pleading and praying.

Only through its mournful windows did the yearning soul dare speak ;

Still through the tears did it ever vainly reach outward some kindred soul to seek.

Unheeding did the ranks sweep by ;

And the weary soul sank back with all its deep unuttered longings to the loneliness of its voiceless world.

Hearing only the measured tread of Guile and Deceit on
　　their sentinel round.
Wherefore was that poor soul of all the host so wounded?
It struggled bravely.
Wherefore was it doomed and prisoned to pine and strive
　　apart?
It battled to the last. Can it be that this captive soul was
　　a changeling, and battled and struggled in a body not its
　　own?
Must Error ever bind the fetters deep into the shrinking
　　flesh?
Will there come no angel to loose them?
And will Truth lift up her lamp at the waking?
Shall the cold tomb of the body grow warm and voice
　　forth all the speechless thought of the soul when the
　　sleeping dead shall rise?
Will there be no uprising in this world?
O! impatient Soul, wait, wait, wait.

II.

"The Angel
Who driveth away the demon band
Bids the din of battle cease."

O prisoned Soul, up in your turrets so high, look down
　　from thy windows to-day!
Dash down the rusty chains of old Error, and unbar the
　　iron doors,
Break the bonds of the Past on the anvil of the Present.
O give me some token for the music that I have sent
　　through your lonely chambers!

Wave but the tip of your white wing in greeting to the Angel that I have sent you!

Look forth on thy fellow Soul pausing at the gate!

List to the sound of his voice that rushes past the red roof, and with unfurled wings, sweeps up its music through the ivory gates to thee!

No other song can thrill its echoes up to thy captive life.

For this Angel hath chilled the hot hand of Sin, and crushed down the grave of the crimson eyes of the Past.

The daylight looms up softly, and feathery Hope is on guard.

O waiting Soul, come forth from your turrets, so lone and high!

Listen to the low sweet music of promise, rushing wildly through floods of God-inspiration of love, up to Eternity.

Tremble not at the bars. Come forth!

The tongue you fear sleeps in frozen silence, and doth thy mighty secret keep.

IN VAIN.

I.

O FOOLISH tears, go back !
Learn to cover your jealous pride far down in the nerveless heart that ye are voices for.

Your sobbings mar the unfinished picture that my trembling life would fill up to greet its dawn.

I know, poor heart, that you are reaching up to a Love that finds not all its demands in thy weak pulse.

And I know that you sob up your red tears to my face, because—because—*others* who care less for his dear Love may, each day, open their glad eyes his lightest wish to bless.

But, jealous heart, *we* will not give him from drops that overflow thy rim.

We will fathom the mysteries of earth, of air and of sea, to fill thy broad life with beauty, and then empty all its very depths of light deep into his wide soul !

II.

Ah ! When I am a cloud—a pliant, floating cloud—I will haunt the Sun-God for some eternal ray of Beauty.

I will wind my soft arms around the wheels of his blazing chariot, till he robes me in gorgeous trains of gold !

I will sing to the stars till they crown me with their richest jewels!

I will plead to the angels for the whitest, broadest wings that ever walled their glorious heights around a dying soul!

Then I will flaunt my light down the steep grooves of space into this dark, old world, until Eyes of Love will brighten for me!

III.

When I am a flower—a wild, sweet flower—I will open my glad blue eyes to one alone.

I will bloom in his footsteps, and muffle their echoes with my velvet lips.

So near him will I grow that his breath shall mark kisses on all my green leaves!

I will fill his deep soul with all the eternal fragrance of my love!

Yes, I will be a violet—a wild sweet violet—and sigh my very life away for him!

IV.

When I am a bird—a white-throated bird—all trimmed in plumage of crimson and gold, I will sing to one alone.

I will come from the sea—the broad blue sea—and fold my wings with olive-leaves to the glad tidings of his hopes!

I will come from the forest—the far old forest—where sighs and tears of reckless loves have never moaned away the morning of poor lives.

I will come from the sky, with songs of an angel, and flutter into his soul to see how I may be all melody to him!

Yes, I will be a bird—a loving, docile bird—and furl my wild wings, and shut my sad eyes in his breast!

V.

When I am a wave—a soft, white wave—I will run up from ocean's purple spheres, and murmur out my low sweet voice to one alone.

I will dash down to the cavern of gems and lift up to his eyes Beauty that will drink light from the Sun!

I will bring blue banners that angels have lost from the clouds.

Yes, I will be a wave—a happy, dancing wave—and leap up in the sunshine to lay my crown of spray-pearls at his feet.

VI.

Alas! poor heart, what am I now?

A weed—a frail, bitter weed—growing outside the garden wall.

All day straining my dull eyes to see the blossoms within, as they wave their crimson flags to the wind.

And yet my dark leaves pray to be as glorious as the rose.

My bitter stalks would be as sweet as the violet if they could.

I try to bloom up into the light.

My poor, yearning soul to Heaven would open its velvet eyes of fire.

Oh ! the love of Beauty through every fibre of my lonely life is trembling !

Every floating cloud and flying bird draws up jealous Envy and bleeding Love !

So passionately wild in me is this burning unspeakable thirst to grow all beauty, all grace, all melody to one—and to him alone !

3

VENETIA.

BRIGHT as the light that burns at night,
 In the starry depths of Aiden,
When star and moon in leafy June
 With love and joy are laden;
Bright as the light from moon and star,
 Stars in glorious cluster,
Be the lights that shine on this life of thine,
 Be the beauty of its lustre.

Beneath the moon in leafy June,
 Sweet vows are fondly spoken;
Beneath the stars, the silvery tune
 Of music floats unbroken.
Beneath the sky, and moon and stars,
 Come nestling birds of beauty,
And Love with Bliss, and Hope with Joy
 Troop down the path of duty.

Oh! ever may'st thou, bird of mine,
 Nestle to my bosom sweetly,
Birds of my soaring, feathery hope,
 That flyeth to me so fleetly.
Oh! ever thus may vows of love
 My yearning soul inherit—
Vows unbroken, as those spoken
 By celestial spirit.

And when the vow thou breathest now,
   For me, for mine and only,
Shall float to Aiden's starry land,
   Where none are lost or lonely,
Believe me, when the angel bends
   His loving ear to listen,
Radiant will be the smile that blends
   With the beauteous tears that glisten.

For darling, those who love us here
   With tender, sweet emotion,
With love that knows no stop or fear,
   But burneth with devotion;
'Tis only but another proof
   That something good is left us,
That we are not by Heaven forgot,
   That Heaven hath not bereft us.

THE SHIP THAT WENT DOWN.

I.

WHO hath not sent out ships to sea?
  Who hath not toiled through light and darkness to
  make them strong for battle?
And how we freighted them with dust from the mountain
  mines!
And red gold, coined from the heart's blood, rich in
  Youth, Love and Beauty!
And we have fondly sent forth on their white decks seven
  times a hundred souls.
Sent them out like sea-girt worlds full of hope, love, care.
  and faith.
O mariners, mariners, watch and beware!

II.

See the Ship that I sent forth!
How proudly she nods her regal head to each saluting
  wave!
How defiantly she flaps her white sails at the sun, who, in
  envy of her beauty, screens his face behind a passing
  cloud, yet never losing sight of her.
The ocean hath deck'd himself in robes of softest blue,
  and lifted his spray-flags to greet her.

The crimson sky hath swooped down from her Heaven-
Palace, and sitteth with her white feet dabbling in the
borders of the sea, while she sendeth sweet promises
on the wings of the wind to my fair Ship.
O mariners, mariners, why did ye not watch and beware?

III.

The faithless sky is black.
The ocean howls on the Ship's rough track.
The strong wind, and the shouting rain swept by like an
armed host whooping out their wild battle-cry.
The tall masts dip their heads down into the deep.
The wet shrouds rattle as they seem to whisper prayers to
themselves;
But the waves leap over their pallid sails, and grapple and
gnaw at their seams.
The poor Ship shrieks and groans out her despair.
She rises up to plead with the sky, and sinks down the
deep valley of water to pray.
O God, make us strong for the battle!

IV.

What says the mariner so hurried and pale?
No need to whisper it, speak out, speak!
Danger and peril you say?
Does your quivering lip and white cheek mean that the
good Ship must go down?
Why stand ye idle and silent?
O sailors, rouse your brave hearts!
Man the rocking masts, and reef the rattling sails!

Heed not the storm-fires that so terribly burn in the black
sky !
Heed not the storm-mad sea below !
Heed not the death-cry of the waves !
Foot to foot, hand to hand !   Toil on brave hearts !

Our good Ship must be saved !
Before us lies the goal !

V.

Too late, too late !
The life-boats are lost.
The rent spars have groaned out their lives, and the white
sails have shrouded them in their rough beds of
Death.
Strong mariners have fainted and failed in the terror and
strife.
White lips are grasping for breath, and trembling out
prayers, and waiting to die.
And the Ship, once so fair, lies a life-freighted wreck.
The Promises, Hopes, and Loves, are sinking, sinking
away.
The winds shriek out their joy, and the waves shout out
their anthem of Death.

Pitiless wind !
Pitiless ocean !

VI.

O mariners, is there no help ?
Is there no beacon-light in the distance ?

Dash the tears of blood from your eyes, and look over
these Alps of water!

See ye no sail glittering through the darkness?

Is there no help?

Must they all die, all die?

So much of Youth, so much of Beauty, so much of Life?

The waves answer with ravenous roar;

They grapple like demons the trembling Ship!

Compassless, rudderless, the poor Ship pleads.

In vain! in vain!

With a struggling, shivering, dying grasp, my good Ship
sank down, down, down to the soundless folds of the
fathomless ocean.

Lost—lost—lost.

BATTLE OF THE STARS.

(After Ossian.)

ALONE on the hill of storms
    The voice of the wind shrieks through the mountain.
The torrent rushes down the rocks.
Red are hundred streams of the light-covered paths of the
    dead.
Shield me in from the storm,
I that am a daughter of the stars, and wear the purple and
    gold of bards, with the badges of Love on my white
    bosom.
I heed not the battle-cry of souls!
I that am chained on this Ossa of existence.
Sorrow hath bound her frozen chain about the wheels of
    my chariot of fire wherein my soul was wont to ride.
Stars, throw off your dark robes, and lead me to the palace
    where my Eros rests on his iron shield of war, his
    gleaming sword in the scabbard, his hounds haunting
    around him.
The water and the storm cry aloud.
I hear not the voice of my Love.
Why delays the chief of the stars his promise?
Here is the terrible cloud, and here the cloud of life with
    its many-colored sides.

Thou didst promise to be with me when night should trail
    her dusky skirts along the borders of my soul.

O wind! O thought! Stream and torrent, be ye silent!

Let the wanderer hear my voice.

Eros, I am waiting. Why delay thy coming? It is Atha
    calls thee.

See the calm moon comes forth.

The flood is silver in the vale.

The rocks are gray on the steep.

I see him not on the mountain brow;

The hounds come not with the glad tidings of his ap-
    proach.

I wait for morning in my tears.

Rear the tomb, but close it not till Eros comes:

Not unharmed will return the eagle from the field of foes.

But Atha will not mark thy wounds, she will be silent in
    her blood.

Love, the great Dreamer, will listen to her voice, and she
    will sleep on the soft bosom of the hills.

O Love! thou Mighty Leveler,

Thou alone canst lay the shepherd's crook beside the
    sceptre,

Thou art the King of the Stars.

Music floats up to thee, receives thy breath, thy burning
    kisses, and comes back with messages to children of
    earth.

Thou art pitiful and bountiful.

Although housed with the golden-haired Son of the Sky,
    with stars for thy children, dwelling in the warm
    clouds, and sleeping on the silver shields of War, yet
    ye do not disdain the lonely Atha that hovers round

the horizon of your Grand Home. You awake and
come forth arrayed in trailing robes of glory, with
blessing and with song to greet her that seeketh thy
mighty presence.

Thy hand giveth Morn her power;

Thy hand lifteth the mist from the hills;

Thy hand createth all of Beauty;

Thy hand giveth Morn her rosy robes;

Thy hands bound up the wounds of Eros after the battle:

Thy hands lifted him to the skirts of the wind, like the
eagle of the forest.

Thy hands have bound his brow with the spoils of the
foe.

Thy hands have given to me the glittering spear, and hel
met of power and might;

Nor settles the darkness on me.

The fields of Heaven are mine.

I will hush the sullen roar of the enemy.

Warriors shall lift their shields to me.

My arm is strong, my sword defends the weak.

I will loose the thong of the Oppressed, and dash to hell
the Oppressor.

A thousand warriors stretch their spears around me.

I battle for the stars.

It was thy hands, O Love, that loosed my golden tresses,
and girded my white limbs in armor, and made me
leader of the armies of Heaven.

Thy voice aroused the sluggard soul.

Thy voice calleth back the sleeping dead.

Thou alone, O Mighty Ruler, canst annihilate space, hush
the shrieking wind, hide the white-haired waves,

and bear me to the arms and burning kisses of my
Eros.

And it is thou who makest beautiful the prison-houses of
earth.

I once was chained to their darkness, but thou, O Love,
brought crimson roses to lay on my pale bosom, and
covered the cold damp walls with the golden shields
of the sun, and left thy purple garments whereon my
weary bleeding feet might rest.

And when black-winged night rolled along the sky, thy
shield covered the moon, and thy hands threw back
the prison-roof, and unfolded the gates of the clouds,
and I slept in the white arms of the stars.

And thou, O Beam of Life! didst thou not forget the
lonely prisoner of Chillon in his gloomy vault? thy
blessed ray of Heaven-light stole in and made glad
his dreams.

Thou hast lifted the deep-gathered mist from the dungeons
of Spielberg;

Ugolino heard thy voice in his hopeless cell:

Thy blessed hand soothed Damiens on his bed of steel;

It is thy powerful hand that lights up to Heaven the inspired life of Garabaldi.

And it is thy undying power that will clothe Italy in the
folds of thy wings, and rend the helmet from the dark
brow of old Austria, and bury her in the eternal tomb
of darkness.

Thou didst not forget children of earth, who roll the waves
of their souls to our ship of the sky.

But men are leagued against us—strong mailed men of
earth,

Around the dwellers in the clouds they rise in wrath.

No words come forth, they seize their blood-stained daggers.

Each takes his hill by night, at intervals they darkly stand counting the power and host of Heaven.

Their black unmuzzled hounds howl their impatience as we come on watch in our glittering armor.

The hills no longer smile up to greet us, they are covered with these tribes of earth leading their war-dogs, and leaving their footprints of blood.

Unequal bursts the hum of voices, and the clang of arms between the roaring wind.

And they dare to blaspheme the very stars, and even God on His high throne in the Heaven of Heavens, by pleading for Love.

Love sacrifices all things to bless the thing it loves, not destroy.

Go back to your scorching homes ;

Go back to your frozen souls ;

Go back to your seas of blood ;

Go back to your chains, your loathsome charnel houses ;

Give us the green bosom of the hills to rest upon ;

Broad over them rose the moon.

O Love, Great Ruler, call upon thy children to buckle on the armor of war, for behold the enemy blackens all earth in waiting for us.

See the glittering of their unsheathed swords.

They bear blood-stained banners of death and destruction.

And, lo, their Leader comes forth on the Pale Horse.

His sword is a green meteor half-extinguished.

His face is without form, and dark withal, dark as the tales
    of other times, before the light of song arose.

Mothers, clasp your new-born children close to your white
    bosoms !

Daughters of the stars, sleep no more, the enemy ap-
    proacheth !

Look to your white shields !

Bind up your golden tresses !

See the blood upon the pale breasts of your sisters.

Where are your banners ?

O sluggards, awake to the call of the Mighty Ruler !

Hear ye not the clash of arms ? Arise around me, chil-
    dren of the Land Unknown.

Up, up, grasp your helmet and your spear !

Let each one look upon her shield as the ruler of War.

Come forth in your purple robes, sound your silver-tongue
    trumpets ;

Rush upon the enemy with your thousand and thousands
    of burnished spears !

Let your voices ring through the Universe, " Liberty,
    liberty for the stars." Thunder it on the ears of the
    guilty and the doomed !

Sound it with the crash of Heaven's wrath to the hearts
    of branded—God-cursed things who have stood up
    and scorned their Maker with laughing curses, as
    they dashed the crown from her brow, and hurled her
    into Hell.

Pray ye not for them, hills !   Heed ye not, O winds, their
    penitence is feigned !

Let your voices, O floods, be hushed ! stars, close your
    mighty flanks, and battle on them !

Chain them down close to the fire!

They were merciless, bind their blood-stained hands.

They are fiends, and if ye loose them they will tear children from their mothers, wives from their husbands, sisters from their brothers, daughters from their fathers.

And these fiends, these children of eternal damnation, these men will tear souls from bodies, and then smear their hands with blood, and laugh as they sprinkle it in the dead up-turned faces of their victims.

It is Atha thy leader that calls to you.

Beat them down, beat them down.

I know these war-dogs.

They strangled my warrior, Eros!

Warrior of my soul;

Warrior of the strong race of Eagles!

His crimson life crushed out on the white sails of a ship.

Battle them down to dust.

Battle them back into their own slimy souls;

Battle them, ye starry armies of Heaven, down into the silent sea of their own blood;

Battle on, the wind is with ye;

Battle on, the sun is with ye;

Battle on, the waves are with ye;

The Angels are with ye;

God is with us!

MYSELF.

" La patience est amère ; mais le fruit en est doux !"

I.

AWAY down into the shadowy depths of the Real I
once lived.

I thought that to seem was to be.

But the waters of Marah were beautiful, yet they were
bitter.

I waited, and hoped, and prayed ;

Counting the heart-throbs and the tears that answered
them.

Through my earnest pleadings for the True, I learned
that the mildest mercy of life was a smiling sneer ;

And that the business of the world was to lash with
vengeance all who dared to be what their God had made
them.

Smother back tears to the red blood of the heart !

Crush out things called souls !

No room for them here !

II.

Now I gloss my pale face with laughter, and sail my
voice on with the tide.

Decked in jewels and lace, I laugh beneath the gas-light's glare, and quaff the purple wine.

But the minor-keyed soul is standing naked and hungry upon one of Heaven's high hills of light.

Standing and waiting for the blood of the feast!

Starving for one poor word!

Waiting for God to launch out some beacon on the boundless shores of this Night.

Shivering for the uprising of some soft wing under which it may creep, lizard-like, to warmth and rest.

Waiting! Starving and shivering!

III.

Still I trim my white bosom with crimson roses; for none shall see the thorns.

I bind my aching brow with a jeweled crown, that none shall see the iron one beneath.

My silver-sandaled feet keep impatient time to the music, because I cannot be calm.

I laugh at earth's passion-fever of Love; yet I know that God is near to the soul on the hill, and hears the ceaseless ebb and flow of a hopeless love, through all my laughter.

But if I can cheat my heart with the old comfort, that love can be forgotten, is it not better?

After all, living is but to play a part!

The poorest worm would be a jewel-headed snake if she could!

IV.

All this grandeur of glare and glitter has its night-time.

The pallid eyelids must shut out smiles and daylight.

Then I fold my cold hands, and look down at the restless rivers of a love that rushes through my life.

Unseen and unknown they tide on over black rocks and chasms of Death.

Oh, for one sweet word to bridge their terrible depths !

O jealous soul ! why wilt thou crave and yearn for what thou canst not have ?

And life is so long—so long.

V.

With the daylight comes the business of living.

The prayers that I sent trembling up the golden thread of hope all come back to me.

I lock them close in my bosom, far under the velvet and roses of the world.

For I know that stronger than these torrents of passion is the soul that hath lifted itself up to the hill.

What care I for his careless laugh ?

I do not sigh ; but I know that God hears the life-blood dripping as I, too, laugh.

I would not be thought a foolish rose, that flaunts her red heart out to the sun.

Loving is not living !

VI.

Yet through all this I know that night will roll back

from the still, gray plain of heaven, and that my triumph shall rise sweet with the dawn !

When these mortal mists shall unclothe the world, then shall I be known as I am !

When I dare be dead and buried behind a wall of wings, then shall he know me !

When this world shall fall, like some old ghost, wrapped in the black skirts of the wind, down into the fathomless eternity of fire, then shall souls uprise !

When God shall lift the frozen seal from struggling voices, then shall we speak !

When the purple-and-gold of our inner natures shall be lighted up in the Eternity of Truth, then will love be mine !

I can wait.

INTO THE DEPTHS.

I.

LOST—lost—lost!
  To me, for ever, the seat near the blood of the
feast.
  To me, for ever, the station near the Throne of Love!
  To me, for ever, the Kingdom of Heaven—and I the
least.

> Oh, the least in love—
> The least in joy—
> The least in life—
> The least in death—
> The least in beauty—
> The least in eternity.

So much of rich, foaming, bubbling human blood drank
down into the everlasting sea of Sin.
  The jasper gates are closed on the crimson highway of
the clouds.

> The Seven Angels stand on guard.
> Seven thunders utter their voices.

And the angels have not sealed up those things which
the seven thunders have uttered.
  I have pleaded to the seventh angel for the little book.
  But he heedeth me not.

All life is bitter, not one drop as sweet as honey.

And yet I prophesy before many people, and nations, and tongues, and kings!

II.

Lost—lost—lost!

The little golden key which the first angel entrusted to me.

The gates are closed, and I may not enter.

Yet arrayed in folds of white, these angels are more terrible to me than the fabled watcher of the Hesperides golden treasures.

Because it is I alone of all God's creatures that am shut out.

For others the bolts are withdrawn, and the little book unsealed.

With wistful eyes, and longing heart, I wander in the distance, waiting for the angels to sleep.

Tremblingly I peer through the gloaming of horrid shadows, and visions of wasted moments.

But the white eyelids of the angels never droop.

In vain I plead to them that it was I who built the throne.

In vain do I tell them that it was I who gemmed it with Faith and Truth, and the dews of my life's morn.

In vain do I tell them that they are my hopes which they stand in solemn guard to watch.

In vain do I plead my right as queen of the starry highway.

In vain do I bind my golden tresses with the pale lilies of the valley.

In vain do I display to them my purple broidered robes, and the silver badge of God's eternal bards that I wear on my white bosom.

In vain do I wind my soft arms around their silver-sandaled feet.

They heed me not.

But point to the whirlpool called the world.

Must the warm, living, loving soul a wanderer be?

Are all its yearnings vain?

Are all its prayings vain?

Will there be no light to guide me?

Will there be strong arm at the helm?

Must the full lamp of life wane so early?

Ah, I see, all is lost—lost—lost!

III.

Deep into the depths!

Struggling all the day-time—weeping all the night-time!

Writing away all vitality.

Talking to people, nations, tongues, and kings that heed me not.

Cast out of my own kingdom on to the barren battle-plain of bloodless life.

A thousand foes advancing?

A thousand weapons glancing!

And I in the sternest scene of strife.

Panting wildly in the race.

Malice and Envy on the track.

Fleet of foot, they front me with their daggers at my breast.

All heedless of my tears and prayers, they tear the white flowers from my brow, and the olive leaves from my breast, and soil with their blood-marked hands the broidered robes of purple beauty.

Life's gems are torn from me, and in scattered fragments around me lie.

All lost—lost—lost!

IV.

Out of the depths have I cried unto thee, O Lord!
Weeping all the night-time.
Weeping sad and chill through the lone woods.
Straying 'mong the ghostly trees.
Wandering through the rustling leaves.
Sobbing to the moon, whose icy light wraps me like a shroud.

Leaning on a hoary rock, praying to the mocking stars.
With Love's o'erwhelming power startling my soul like an earthquake shock.

I lift my voice above the low howl of the winds to call my Eros to come and give me light and life once more.

His broad arms can raise me up to the light, and his red lips can kiss me back to life.

I heed not the storm of the world, nor the clashing of its steel.

I wait—wait—wait!

V.

How can I live so deep into the depths with all this wealth of love?

Oh, unspeakable, passionate fire of love !

> Cold blood heedeth ye not.
>
> Cold eyes know ye not.

But in this wild soul of seething passion we have warmed together.

I feel thy lava tide dashing recklessly through every blue course !

Grand, beauteous Love !

Let us live alone, far from the world of battle and pain, where we can forget this grief that has plunged me into the depths.

We will revel in ourselves.

Come, Eros, thou creator of this divine passion, come and lay my weary head on your bosom.

Draw me close up to your white breast and lull me to sleep.

Smooth back the damp, tangled mass from my pale brow.

> I am so weary of battle—
>
> Take this heavy shield.
>
> I am so weary of toil—
>
> Loosen my garments.

Now, wrap me close in your bosom to rest.

Closer—closer still !

Let your breath warm my cold face.

This is life—this is love !

Oh, kiss me till I sleep—till I sleep—I sleep.

SALE OF SOULS.

I.

OH, I am wild—wild!
 Angels of the weary-hearted, come to thy child.
Spread your white wings over me!
    Tenderly, tenderly,
    Lovingly, lovingly,
    Plead for me, plead for me!

II.

Souls for sale! souls for sale!
Souls for gold! who'll buy?
In the pent-up city, through the wild rush and beat of
 human hearts, I hear this unceasing, haunting cry:
    Souls for sale! souls for sale!
    Through mist and gloom,
    Through hate and love,
    Through peace and strife,
    Through wrong and right,
    Through life and death,
The hoarse voice of the world echoes up the cold gray
 sullen river of life.
    On, on, on!

No silence until it shall have reached the solemn sea of
    God's for ever ;
              No rest, no sleep ;
Waking through the thick gloom of midnight, to hear the
    damning cry as it mingles and clashes with the rough
    clang of gold.
              Poor Heart, poor Heart,
              Alas ! I know thy fears.

III.

The hollow echoes that the iron-shod feet of the years
    throw back on the sea of change still vibrate through
    the grave-yard of prayers and tears ;—
              Prayers that fell unanswered,
              Tears that followed hopelessly.
But pale Memory comes back through woe and shame
    and strife, bearing on her dark wings their buried
    voices ;
Like frail helpless barks, they wail through the black sea
    of the crowded city,
              Mournfully, mournfully.

IV.

Poor Heart, what do the waves say to thee ?
The sunshine laughed on the hill sides.
The link of years that wore a golden look bound me to
    woman-life by the sweet love of my Eros, and the
    voice of one who made music to call me mother.
Weak Heart, weak Heart !

Oh, now I reel madly on through clouds and storms and
　　night.

The hills have grown dark,

They lack the grace of my golden-haired child, to climb
　　their steep sides, and bear me their smiles in the
　　blue-eyed violets of our spring-time.

Sad Heart, what do the hills say to thee?

They speak of my Eros, and how happily in the dim dis-
　　colored hours we dreamed away the glad light, and
　　watched the gray robes of night as she came through
　　the valley, and ascended on her way to the clouds.

　　　　　　Kisses of joy, and kisses of life,
　　　　　　Kisses of heaven, and kisses of earth,

Clinging and clasping white hands;

Mingling of soft tresses;

Murmurings of love, and murmurings of life,

With the warm blood leaping up in joy to answer its
　　music;

The broad shelter of arms wherein dwelt peace and con-
　　tent, so sweet to love.

All, all were mine.

　　　　　　Loving Heart, loving Heart,

Hush the wailing and sobbing voice of the past;

Sleep in thy rivers of the soul,

　　　　　　Poor Heart.

V.

Souls for sale!

The wild cry awoke the god of ambition, that slumbered
　　in the bosom of Eros;

From out the tents he brought forth his shield and spear,
     to see them smile back at the sun ;

Clad in armor, he went forth to the cities of the world,
     where brave men battle for glory, and souls are bar-
     tered for gold.

Weeping and fearing, haggard and barefoot, I clung to him
     with my fainting child.

Weary miles of land and water lay in their waste around
     us,

We reached the sea of the city.

Marble towers lifted their proud heads beyond the scope
     of vision.

Wild music mingled with laughter.

The tramp of hoofs on the iron streets, and the cries of the
     drowning, and the curses of the damned were all heard
     in that Babel, where the souls of men can be bought
     for gold.

All the air seemed dark with evil wings.

And all that was unholy threw their shadows everywhere,

         Shadows on the good,

         Shadows on the bad,

         Shadows on the lowly,

         Shadows on the lost !

All tossing upon the tide of rushing, restless destiny ;

Upon all things written :

         Souls for sale !

         Lost Heart, lost Heart !

VI.

A soul mantled in glory, and sold to the world ;

O horrible sale !
O seal of blood !
Give back my Eros.

His bowstring still sounds on the blast, yet his arrow was broken in the fall.

Oh leave me not on the wreck of this dark-bosomed ship while Eros lies pale on the rocks of the world.

Driven before the furious gale by the surging ocean's strife ;

The strong wind lifting up the sounding sail, and whistling through the ropes and masts ; waves lash the many-colored sides of the ship, dash her against the oozy rocks.

The strength of old ocean roars.

The low booming of the signal gun is heard above the tempest.

Oh how many years must roll their slow length along my life, ere the land be in sight !

When will the morning dawn ?
When will the clouds be light ?
When will the storm be hushed ?
It is so dark and cold.
Angels of the weary-hearted, come to your child !
Build your white wings around me.

Tenderly, tenderly,
Pity me, pity me.

ONE YEAR AGO.

IN feeling I was but a child,
    When first we met—one year ago,
As free and guileless as the bird,
    That roams the dreary woodland through.

My heart was all a pleasant world
    Of sunbeams dewed with April tears:
Life's brightest page was turned to me,
    And naught I read of doubts or fears.

We met—we loved—one year ago,
    Beneath the stars of summer skies;
Alas! I knew not then, as now,
    The darkness of life's mysteries.

You took my hand—one year ago,
    Beneath the azure dome above,
And gazing on the stars you told
    The trembling story of your love.

I gave to you—one year ago,
    The only jewel that was mine;
My heart took off her lonely crown,
    And all her riches gave to thine.

You loved me, too, when first we met,
　　Your tender kisses told me so.
How changed you are from what you were
　　In life and love—one year ago.

With mocking words and cold neglect,
　　My truth and passion are repaid,
And of a soul, once fresh with love,
　　A dreary desert you have made.

Why did you fill my youthful life
　　With such wild dreams of hope and bliss?
Why did you say you loved me then,
　　If it were all to end in this?

You robbed me of my faith and trust
　　In all Life's beauty—Love and Truth,
You left me nothing—nothing save
　　A hopeless, blighted, dreamless youth.

Strike if you will, and let the stroke
　　Be heavy as my weight of woe;
I shall not shrink, my heart is cold,
　　'Tis broken since one year ago.

GENIUS.

" Where'er there's a life to be kindled by love,
    Wherever a soul to inspire,
Strike this key-note of God that trembles above
    Night's silver-tongued voices of fire."

GENIUS is power.

The power that grasps in the universe, that dives out beyond space, and grapples with the starry worlds of heaven.

If genius achieves nothing, shows us no results, it is so much the less genius.

The man who is constantly fearing a lion in his path is a coward.

The man or woman whom excessive caution holds back from striking the anvil with earnest endeavor, is poor and cowardly of purpose.

The required step must be taken to reach the goal, though a precipice be the result.

Work must be done, and the result left to God.

The soul that is in earnest, will not stop to count the cost.

Circumstances cannot control genius : it will nestle with them : its power will bend and break them to its path.

This very audacity is divine.

Jesus of Nazareth did not ask the consent of the high priests in the temple when he drove out the "money-changers;" but, impelled by inspiration, he knotted the cords and drove them hence.

Genius will find room for itself, or it is none.

Men and women, in all grades of life, do their utmost.

If they do little, it is because they have no capacity to do more.

I hear people speak of "unfortunate genius," of "poets who never penned their inspirations;" that

"Some mute inglorious Milton here may rest;"

of "unappreciated talent," and "malignant stars," and other contradictory things.

It is all nonsense.

Where power exists, it cannot be suppressed any more than the earthquake can be smothered.

As well attempt to seal up the crater of Vesuvius as to hide God's given power of the soul.

"You may as well forbid the mountain pines
To wag their high tops, and to make no noise
When they are fretten with the gusts of heaven,"

as to hush the voice of genius.

There is no such thing as unfortunate genius.

If a man or woman is fit for work, God appoints the field.

He does more; He points to the earth with her mountains, oceans, and cataracts, and says to man, "*Be great!*"

He points to the eternal dome of heaven and its blazing worlds, and says : "Bound out thy life with beauty."

He points to the myriads of down-trodden, suffering men and women, and says : "Work with me for the redemption of these, my children."

He lures, and incites, and thrusts greatness upon men, and they will not take the gift.

Genius, on the contrary, loves toil, impediment, and poverty ; for from these it gains its strength, throws off the shadows, and lifts its proud head to immortality.

Neglect is but the fiat to an undying future.

To be popular is to be endorsed in the To-day and forgotten in the To-morrow.

It is the mess of pottage that alienates the birthright.

Genius that succumbs to misfortune, that allows itself to be blotted by the slime of slander—and other serpents that infest society—is so much the less genius.

The weak man or woman who stoops to whine over neglect, and poverty, and the snarls of the world, gives the sign of his or her own littleness.

Genius is power.

The eternal power that can silence worlds with its voice, and battle to the death ten thousand arméd Hercules.

Then make way for this God-crowned Spirit of Night, that was born in that Continuing City, but lives in lowly and down-trodden souls !

Fling out the banner !

Its broad folds of sunshine will wave over turret and dome, and over the thunder of oceans on to eternity.

5

"Fling it out, fling it out o'er the din of the world!
    Make way for this banner of flame,
That streams from the mast-head of ages unfurled,
    And inscribed by the deathless in name.
And thus through the years of eternity's flight,
    This insignia of soul shall prevail,
The centre of glory, the focus of light;
    O Genius! proud Genius, all hail!"

DRIFTS THAT BAR MY DOOR.

I.

O ANGELS! will ye never sweep the drifts from my
door?

Will ye never wipe the gathering rust from the hinges?

How long must I plead and cry in vain?

Lift back the iron bars, and lead me hence.

Is there not a land of peace beyond my door?

Oh, lead me to it—give me rest—release me from this
unequal strife.

Heaven can attest that I fought bravely when the heavy
blows fell fast.

Was it my sin that strength failed?

Was it my sin that the battle was in vain?

Was it my sin that I lost the prize? I do not sorrow
for all the bitter pain and blood it cost me.

Why do ye stand sobbing in the sunshine?

I cannot weep.

There is no sunlight in this dark cell. I am starving
for light.

O angels! sweep the drifts away—unbar my door!

II.

Oh, is this all?

Is there nothing more of life?

See how dark and cold my cell.

The pictures on the walls are covered with mould.

The earth-floor is slimy with my wasting blood.

The embers are smouldering in the ashes.

The lamp is dimly flickering, and will soon starve for oil in this horrid gloom.

My wild eyes paint shadows on the walls.

And I hear the poor ghost of my lost love moaning and sobbing without.

Shrieks of my unhappiness are borne to me on the wings of the wind.

I sit cowering in fear, with my tattered garments close around my choking throat.

I move my pale lips to pray; but my soul has lost her wonted power.

Faith is weak.

Hope has laid her whitened corse upon my bosom.

The lamp sinks lower and lower. O angels! sweep the drifts away—unbar my door!

III.

Angels, is this my reward?

Is this the crown ye promised to set down on the foreheads of the loving—the suffering—the deserted?

Where are the sheaves I toiled for?

Where the golden grain ye promised?

These are but withered leaves.

Oh, is this all?

Meekly I have toiled and spun the fleece.

All the work ye assigned, my willing hands have accomplished.

See how thin they are, and how they bleed.

Ah me! what meagre pay, e'en when the task is over!

My fainting child, whose golden head graces e'en **this** dungeon, looks up to me and pleads for life.

O God! my heart is breaking!

Despair and Death have forced their skeleton **forms** through the grated window of my cell, and stand clamoring for their prey.

The lamp is almost burnt out.

Angels, sweep the drifts away—unbar my door!

IV.

Life is a lie, and Love a cheat.

There is a graveyard in my poor heart—dark, heaped-up graves, from which no flowers spring.

The walls are so high, that the trembling wings of birds do break ere they reach the summit, and they fall, wounded, and die in my bosom.

I wander 'mid the gray old tombs, and talk with the ghosts of my buried hopes.

They tell me of my Eros, and how they fluttered around him, bearing sweet messages of my love, until one day, with his strong arm, he struck them dead at his feet.

Since then, these poor lonely ghosts have haunted me night and day, for it was I who decked them in my crimson heart-tides, and sent them forth in chariots of fire.

Every breath of wind bears me their shrieks and groans.

I hasten to their graves, and tear back folds and folds

of their shrouds, and try to pour into their cold, nerveless veins the quickening tide of life once more.

Too late—too late !

Despair hath driven back Death, and clasps me in his black arms.

And the lamp ! See, the lamp is dying out !

O angels ! sweep the drifts from my door !—lift up the bars !

V.

Oh, let me sleep.

I close my weary eyes to think—to dream.

Is this what dreams are woven of ?

I stand on the brink of a precipice, with my shivering child strained to my bare bosom.

A yawning chasm lies below.   My trembling feet are on the brink.

I hear again *his* voice ; but he reacheth not out his hand to save me.

Why can I not move my lips to pray ?

They are cold.

My soul is dumb, too.

Death hath conquered !

I feel his icy fingers moving slowly along my heart-strings.

How cold and stiff !

The ghosts of my dead hopes are closing around me.

They stifle me.

They whisper that Eros has come back to me.

But I only see a skeleton wrapped in blood-stained cerements.

There are no lips to kiss me back to life.

O ghosts of Love, move back—give me air !

Ye smell of the dusty grave.

Ye have pressed your cold hands upon my eyes until they are eclipsed.

The lamp has burnt out.

O angels ! be quick ! Sweep the drifts away !—unbar my door !

Oh, light ! light !

ASPIRATION.

POOR, impious Soul! that fixes its high hopes
    In the dim distance, on a throne of clouds,
And from the morning's mist would make the ropes
    To draw it up amid acclaim of crowds—
Beware!   That soaring path is lined with shrouds ;
    And he who braves it, though of sturdy breath,
May meet, half way, the avalanche and death!

O poor young Soul!—whose year-devouring glance
    Fixes in ecstasy upon a star,
Whose feverish brilliance looks a part of earth,
    Yet quivers where the feet of angels are,
And seems the future crown in realms afar—
    Beware !   A spark *thou* art, and dost but see
Thine own reflection in Eternity!

MISERIMUS.

" Sounding through the silent dimness
Where I faint and weary lay,
Spake a poet : ' I will lead thee
To the land of song to-day.' "

I.

O BARDS ! weak heritors of passion and of pain !
Dwellers in the shadowy Palace of Dreams !
With your unmated souls flying insanely at the stars !

Why have you led me lonely and desolate to the Death-
less Hill of Song ?

You promised that I should ring trancing shivers of
rapt melody down to the dumb earth.

You promised that its echoes should vibrate till Time's
circles met in old Eternity.

You promised that I should gather the stars like blossoms to my white bosom.

You promised that I should create a new moon of
Poesy.

You promised that the wild wings of my soul should
shimmer through the dusky locks of the clouds, like
burning arrows, down into the deep heart of the dim
world.

But, O Bards ! sentinels on the Lonely Hill, why breaks
there yet no Day to me ?

II.

O lonely watchers for the Light! how long must I grope
with my dead eyes in the sand?

Only the red fire of Genius, that narrows up life's
chances to the black path that crawls on to the dizzy
clouds.

The wailing music that spreads its pinions to the
tremble of the wind, has crumbled off to silence.

From the steep ideal the quivering soul falls in its
lonely sorrow like an unmated star from the blue heights
of Heaven into the dark sea.

O Genius! is this thy promise?

O Bards! is this all?

A MEMORY.

I SEE her yet, that dark-eyed one,
  Whose bounding heart God folded up
In His, as shuts when day is done,
  Upon the elf the blossom's cup.
On many an hour like this we met,
  And as my lips did fondly greet her,
I blessed her as love's amulet:
  Earth hath no treasure, dearer, sweeter.

The stars that look upon the hill,
  And beckon from their homes at night,
Are soft and beautiful, yet still
  Not equal to her eyes of light.
They have the liquid glow of earth,
  The sweetness of a summer even,
As if some Angel at their birth
  Had dipped them in the hues of Heaven.

They may not seem to others sweet,
  Nor radiant with the beams above,
When first their soft, sad glances meet
  The eyes of those not born for love ;
Yet when on me their tender beams
  Are turned, beneath love's wide control,
Each soft, sad orb of beauty seems
  To look through mine into my soul.

I see her now that dark-eyed one,
    Whose bounding heart God folded up
In His, as shuts when day is done,
    Upon the elf the blossom's cup.
Too late we met, the burning brain,
    The aching heart alone can tell,
How filled our souls of death and pain
    When came the last, sad word, *Farewell!*

HEMLOCK IN THE FURROWS.

I.

O CROWNLESS soul of Ishmael!
 Uplifting and unfolding the white tent of dreams against the sunless base of eternity!

Looking up through thy dumb desolation for white hands to reach out over the shadows, downward, from the golden bastions of God's eternal Citadel!

Praying for Love to unloose the blushing bindings of his nimble shaft and take thee up to his fullest fruition!

Poor Soul! hast thou no prophecy to gauge the distance betwixt thee and thy crown?

Thy crown?

Alas! there is none.

Only a golden-rimmed shadow that went before thee, marking in its tide barren shoals and dust.

At last resting its bright length down in the valley of tears.

Foolish soul! let slip the dusty leash.

Cease listening along the borders of a wilderness for the lost echoes of life.

Drift back through the scarlet light of Memory into the darkness once more.

A corpse hath not power to feel the tying of its hands.

II.

To-night, O Soul! shut off thy little rimmings of Hope, and let us go back to our hemlock that sprang up in the furrows.

Let us go back with bleeding feet and try to break up the harvestless ridges where we starved.

Let us go down to the black sunset whose wings of fire burnt out thy flowery thickets of Day, and left a Night to swoop down the lonesome clouds to thee.

Go back to the desolate time when the dim stars looked out from Heaven, filmy and blank, like eyes in the wide front of some dead beast.

Go, press thy nakedness to the burnt, bare rocks, under whose hot, bloodless ribs the River of Death runs black with human sorrow.

To-night, O Soul! fly back through all the grave-yards of thy Past.

Fly back to them this night with thy fretful wings, even though their bloody breadth must wrestle long against Hell's hollow bosom!

III.

Jealous Soul!

The stars that are trembling forth their silent messages to the hills have none for thee!

The mother-moon that so lovingly reacheth down her arms of light heedeth not thy Love!

See, the pale pinions that thou hast pleaded for gather themselves up into rings and then slant out to the dust!

The passion-flowers lift up their loving faces and open

their velvet lips to the baptism of Love, but heed not thy warm kisses !

Shut out all this brightness that hath God's Beauty and liveth back the silence of His Rest.

Cease knocking at the starry gate of the wondrous realm of Song.

Hush away this pleading and this praying.

Go back to thy wail of fetter and chain !

Go back to thy night of loving in vain !

IV.

O weak Soul ! let us follow the heavy hearse that bore our old Dream out past the white-horned Daylight of Love.

Let thy pale Dead come up from their furrows of winding-sheets to mock thy prayers with what thy days might have been.

Let the Living come back and point out the shadows they swept o'er the disk of thy morning star.

Have thou speech with them for the story of its swimming down in tremulous nakedness to the Red Sea of the Past.

Go back and grapple with thy lost Angels that stand in terrible judgment against thee.

Seek thou the bloodless skeleton once hugged to thy depths.

Hath it grown warmer under thy passionate kissings ?

Or, hath it closed its seeming wings and shrunk its white body down to a glistening coil ?

Didst thou wait the growth of fangs to front the arrows of Love's latest peril ?

Didst thou not see a black, hungry vulture wheeling down low to the white-bellied coil where thy Heaven had once based itself?

O blind Soul of mine!

V.

Blind, blind with tears!

Not for thee shall Love climb the Heaven of thy columned Hopes to Eternity!

Under the silver shadow of the cloud waits no blushing star thy tryst.

Didst thou not see the pale, widowed West loose her warm arms and slide the cold burial earth down upon the bare face of thy sun?

Gazing upon a shoal of ashes, thou hast lost the way that struck upon the heavy, obstructive valves of the grave to thy Heaven.

Mateless thou needs must vaguely feel along the dark, cold steeps of Night.

Hath not suffering made thee wise?

When, oh when?

VI.

Go down to the black brink of Death and let its cool waters press up to thy weary feet.

See if its trembling waves will shatter the grand repeating of thy earth-star.

See if the eyes that said to thee their speechless Love so close will reach thee from this sorrowful continent of Life.

See if the red hands that seamed thy shroud will come around thy grave.

Then, O Soul! thou mayst drag them to the very edges of the Death-pit, and shake off their red shadows!

Thy strong vengeance may then bind the black-winged crew down level with their beds of fire!

VII.

But wait, wait!

Take up the ruined cup of Life that struck like a planet through the dark, and shone clear and full as we starved for the feast within.

Go down to the black offings of the Noiseless Sea, and wait, poor Soul!

Measure down the depth of thy bitterness and wait!

Bandage down with the grave-clothes the pulses of thy dying life and wait!

Wail up thy wild, desolate echoes to the pitying arms of God and wait!

Wait, wait!

6

HEAR, O ISRAEL!

(From the Hebrew.)

"And they shall be my people, and I will be their God."—JEREMIAH
xxxii. 38.

I.

HEAR, O Israel! and plead my cause against the
ungodly nation!

'Midst the terrible conflict of Love and Peace, I departed from thee, my people, and spread my tent of many
colors in the land of Egypt.

In their crimson and fine linen I girded my white form.

Sapphires gleamed their purple light from out the darkness of my hair.

The silver folds of their temple foot-cloth was spread
beneath my sandaled feet.

Thus I slumbered through the daylight.

   Slumbered 'midst the vapor of sin,
   Slumbered 'midst the battle and din,
   Wakened 'midst the strangle of breath,
   Wakened 'midst the struggle of death!

II.

Hear, O Israel! my people—to thy goodly tents do I
return with unstained hands.

Like as the harts for the water-brooks, in thirst, do pant and bray, so pants and cries my longing soul for the house of Jacob.

My tears have unto me been meat, both in night and day:

And the crimson and fine linen moulders in the dark tents of the enemy.

With bare feet and covered head do I return to thee, O Israel!

With sackcloth have I bound the hem of my garments.

With olive leaves have I trimmed the border of my bosom.

The breaking waves did pass o'er me; yea, were mighty in their strength—

Strength of the foe's oppression.

My soul was cast out upon the waters of Sin: but it has come back to me.

My transgressions have vanished like a cloud.

The curse of Balaam hath turned to a blessing;

And the doors of Jacob turn not on their hinges against me.

Rise up, O Israel! for it is I who passed through the fiery furnace seven times, and come forth unscathed, to redeem thee from slavery, O my nation! and lead thee back to God.

III.

Brothers mine, fling out your white banners over this Red Sea of wrath!

Hear ye not the Death-cry of a thousand burning, bleeding wrongs?

Against the enemy lift thy sword of fire, even thou, O Israel! whose prophet I am.

For I, of all thy race, with these tear-blinded eyes, still see the watch-fire leaping up its blood-red flame from the ramparts of our Jerusalem!

And my heart alone beats and palpitates, rises and falls with the glimmering and the gleaming of the golden beacon flame, by whose light I shall lead thee, O my people! back to freedom!

Give me time—oh give me time to strike from your brows the shadow-crowns of Wrong!

On the anvil of my heart will I rend the chains that bind ye.

Look upon me—oh look upon me, as I turn from the world—from love, and passion, to lead thee, thou Chosen of God, back to the pastures of Right and Life!

Fear me not; for the best blood that heaves this heart now runs for thee, thou Lonely Nation!

Why wear ye not the crown of eternal royalty, that God set down upon your heads?

Back, tyrants of the red hands!

Slouch back to your ungodly tents, and hide the Cain-brand on your foreheads!

Life for life, blood for blood, is the lesson ye teach us.

We, the Children of Israel, will not creep to the kennel graves ye are scooping out with iron hands, like scourged hounds!

Israel! rouse ye from the slumber of ages, and, though Hell welters at your feet, carve a road through these tyrants!

The promised dawn-light is here ; and God—O the God
of our nation is calling !

Press on—press on !

IV.

Ye, who are kings, princes, priests, and prophets. Ye
men of Judah and bards of Jerusalem, hearken unto my
voice, and I will speak thy name, O Israel !

Fear not ; for God hath at last let loose His thinkers,
and their voices now tremble in the mighty depths of this
old world !

Rise up from thy blood-stained pillows !

Cast down to dust the hideous, galling chains that bind
thy strong hearts down to silence !

Wear ye the badge of slaves ?

See ye not the watch-fire ?

Look aloft, from thy wilderness of thought !

Come forth with the signs and wonders, and thy strong
hands, and stretched-out arms, even as thou didst from
Egypt !

Courage, courage ! trampled hearts !

Look at these pale hands and frail arms, that have rent
asunder the welded chains that an army of the Philistines
bound about me !

But the God of all Israel set His seal of fire on my
breast, and lighted up, with inspiration, the soul that pants
for the Freedom of a nation !

With eager wings she fluttered above the blood-stained
bayonet-points of the millions, who are trampling upon
the strong throats of God's people.

Rise up, brave hearts !

The sentry cries : " All's well !" from Hope's tower !
Fling out your banners of Right !
The watch fire grows brighter !
   All's well ! All's well !
   Courage ! Courage !
The Lord of Hosts is in the field,
The God of Jacob is our shield !

WHERE THE FLOCKS SHALL BE LED.

WHERE shall I lead the flocks to-day?
Is there no Horeb for me beyond this desert?

Is there no rod with which I can divide this sea of blood to escape mine enemies?

Must I pine in bondage and drag these heavy chains through the rocky path of my unrecompensed toil?

Must I, with these pale, feeble hands, still lift the wreathed bowl for others to drink, while my lips are parched and my soul unslaked?

Must I hold the light above my head that others may find the green pastures as they march in advance, whilst I moan and stumble with my bare feet tangled and clogged with this load of chains?

Must I still supply the lamp with oil that gives no light to me?

Shall I reck not my being's wane in these long days of bondage and struggle?

Is there no time for me to pray?

Others are climbing the hill-side of glory whilst I am left to wrestle with darkness in the valley below.

Oh where shall I lead the flocks to-day?

Once the soft white flowers of love bloomed upon my bosom.

But, oh! see this iron crown hath crushed the purple blood from my temples until the roses are drowned in it and 'tis withered and weeping on my breast.

The dear hands that planted the sweet flowers should not have been the ones to clasp this heavy iron band round my aching head.

Oh why is it that those we love and cling to with the deepest adoration of our unschooled natures should be the first to whet the steel and bury it in the warm blood that passionate love had created?

Answer me, ye who are ranged mockingly around me with your unsheathed knives. Answer me.

I know that ye are waiting to strike, but answer me first.

I know that if my tearful eyes do but wander from ye one moment, your trembling cowardly hands will strike the blow that your black souls are crying out for.

But let your haggard lips speak to give me warning.

Ye wait to see if these tears will blind me.

But I shall not plead for mercy.

Weak and fainting as I am, I fear you not.

For, lo! behold!

I bare to you my white mother bosom!

See, I draw from my heart a dagger whose blade is keener than any ye can hold against me.

The hands I loved most whetted it, and struck with fatal precision ye never can, for he knew where the heart lay.

No one else can ever know.

Look how the thick blood slowly drips from the point of the blade and sinks into the sand at my feet.

The white sand rolls over and covers the stains.

Flowers will spring up even there.

One day the sands will loose their seal, and they will speak.

The first shall be last and the last shall be first.

The first is my own life and the last my child.

That one will bloom eternally.

And together we will sound the horn that shall herd the flocks and lead them up to the Father's pastures.

For I know that somewhere there grows a green bush in the crevice of a rock, and that the enemy's foot may not crush it nor his hand uproot it.

A golden gate shall be unloosed, and we shall feed upon the freshness of the mountains.

But, see, the furnace has been heated seven times.

I still stand barefoot and bondage-bound, girt around my warriors, and chained and down-trodden upon these burning sands.

And yet I will escape.

Look, the pillar of cloud is over my head.

He who saved the bush on Horeb from the flames can lead me through the Red Sea, beyond the reach of these Egyptians with their rumbling chariots, tramping steeds, clashing weapons, and thunders of war.

Above the tumult I hear the voice of Aaron.

When the sun rises the chains shall be unsealed.

The blood shall be lifted from the earth and will speak.

The task-masters shall perish.

The white flocks shall be led back to the broad plains of Hebron.

I still see the pillar of cloud.

God is in the midst of us !

PRO PATRIA.

AMERICA, 1861.

GOD'S armies of Heaven, with pinions extended,
　　Spread wide their white arms to the standard of
　　　　Light;
And bending far down to the great Heart of Nature,
　　With kisses of Love drew us up from the Night.

Proud soul of the Bondless! whose stars fleck with crim-
　　son,
　　And warm dreams of gold ev'ry pillar and dome,
That strengthens and crowns the fair temples upswelling
　　To glitter, far-seen, in our Liberty's home—

The spirits of Heroes and Sires of the People,
　　Leaned down from the battlements guarding the world;
To breathe for your Destiny omens of glory
　　And freedom eternal, in Honor impearled.

The storm-goaded mountains, and trees that had battled
　　With winds sweeping angrily down through the years,
Turned red in the blood of the roses of Heaven,
　　'Neath fires lit by sunset on vanishing spears.

The soft Beam of Peace bronzed the rocks of stern ages,
　　And crept from the valley to burn on the spire;

And stooped from the glimmer of gems in the palace,
  To glow in the hovel a soul-heating fire.

Each turret, and terrace, and archway of grandeur,
  Its beauty up-rounded through laughs of the light;
And world-crown'd America chose for her standard
  The blush of the Day and the eyes of the Night.

Then Liberty's sceptre, its last jewel finding,
  Was waved by a God o'er the years to be born,
And far in the future there rusted and crumbled
  The chains of the centuries, ne'er to be worn.

The wave-hosts patrolling the sullen Atlantic,
  With helmets of snow, and broad silvery shields,
Ran clamoring up to the seed-sown embrasures,
  And fashioned new dews for the buds of the fields :

They spread their scroll shields for the breast of Columbia,
  And turned their storm-swords to the enemy's fleet;
Their glory to humble the tyrant that braved them,
  Their honor to lave fair America's feet !

No hot hand of Mars scattered red bolts of thunder
  From out the blest land on their message-wind's breath ;
But softly the murmur of Peace wantoned o'er them,
  And soothed War to sleep in the Cradle of Death,

Then hiding their snow plumes, they slept in their armor,
  And as the sun shone on their crystalline mail ;
Lo! Freedom beheld, from her mountains, a mirror,
  And caught her own image spread under a sail !

So, blest was Columbia ; the focus of Nature's
   Best gifts, and the dimple where rested God's smile ;
The Queen of the World in her young strength and beauty,
   The pride of the skies in her freedom from guile.

Aloft on the mount of God's liberty endless,
   Half-veiled by the clouds of His temple she stood,
Arrayed in the glory of Heaven, the mortal,
   With vigor Immortal unchained in her blood.

A bright helm of stars on her white brow was seated,
   And gold were the plumes from its clusters that fell
To light the gaunt faces of slaves in old kingdoms,
   And show them the way to the hand they loved well.

No gorget of steel rested on her bare bosom,
   Where glittered a necklace of gems from the skies ;
And girding her waist was the red band of sunset,
   With light intertwined 'neath the glance of her eyes.

The sword that had bridged in the dark time of trouble,
   Her heart's grand Niagara rolling in blood ;
Still sheathless she held ; but it turned to a sunbeam,
   And blessed what it touched, like a finger of God !

The robes of her guardian Angels swept round her,
   And flashed through the leaves of the grand Tree of
      Life,
Till all the sweet birds in its depths woke to music,
   And e'en the bruised limbs with new being were rife.

The Eagle's gray eyes, from the crag by the ocean,
   Undazed by the sun, saw the vision of love,

And swift on the rim of the shield of Columbia,
　　The bold Eagle fell from the white throne of Jove ﹐

Columbia ! My Country ! My Mother ! thy glory
　　Was born in a spirit Immortal, divine ;
And when from God's lips passed the nectar of heaven,
　　Thy current baptismal was deified wine !

Thou born of Eternal ! the hand that would harm thee
　　Must wither to dust, and in dust be abhorred,
For thine is the throne whose blue canopy muffles
　　The footfalls of angels, the steps of the Lord !

But hush ! 'Twas the flap of the raven's dark pinions
　　That sounded in woe on the breeze as it passed ;
There cometh a hum, as of distance-veiled battle,
　　From out the deep throat of the quivering blast ;

There cometh a sound like the moan of a lost one
　　From out the red jaws of Hell's cavern of Death ;
The Eagle's strong wing feels the talon of Discord,
　　And all the fair sunlight goes out with a breath !

And see how the purple-hued hills and the valleys
　　Are dark with bent necks and with arms all unnerved ;
And black, yelling hounds bay the soul into madness—
　　The Huntsman of Hell drives the pack that has swerved !

The pale steeds of Death shake the palls of their saddles,
　　And spread their black manes, wrought of shrouds, to
　　　　the wind,
The curst sons of Discord each courser bestriding,
　　To guide the Arch-Demon, who lingers behind

They thunder in rage, o'er the red path of Battle,
  Far up the steep mount where fair Liberty keeps
The soul of a Tyrant in parchment imprisoned;
  God pity us all, if her Sentinel sleeps!

Our Father in Heaven! the shadow of fetters
  Is held in the shade of the Dove's little wing;
And must it again on our smothered hearts settle?
  Peace slain—and the knell of our Honor they ring!

Behold! from the night-checkered edge of the woodland
  A wall of red shields crowdeth into the land,
Their rims shooting horror and bloody confusion,
  Their fields spreading darkness on every hand.

A forest of morions utter grim murder—
  Threats kissed by the sun from their long tongues of steel;
Lo, forests of spears hedge the heart of Columbia,
  And soon their keen points her fair bosom may feel!

Her Cain-branded foes!   How they crawl in the valley,
  And creep o'er the hills, in their dastardly fear!
Afraid, lest their victim should suddenly waken
  And blast them for e'er with a womanly tear!

Like hunters who compass the African jungle,
  Where slumbers Numidia's lion by day,
They falter and pale, looking back at each other,
  And some, in their falsehood, to Providence pray!

Assassins of Liberty! comes there not o'er you
  A thought of the time, when the land you would blight,

Though slumbering 'mid tombs of a hundred dead nations,
  Though Britain's steel bulwarks broke into the light?

And can ye forget the hot blood-rain that deluged
  The Hearts of the Fathers, who left to your care
The beautiful Trust now in slumber before you,
  They starved, fought, and fell to preserve from a snare?

Would ye splash, in your madness, the blood of the children,
  With merciless blows, in the poor mother's face?
Turn back, ye Assassins! or wear on your foreheads
  For ever the brand of a God-hated race!

Down, down to the dust with ye, cowards inhuman!
  And learn, as ye grovel, for mercy to live,
That Love is the Sceptre and Throne of the Nation,
  And Freedom the Crown that the centuries give!

Unrighteous Ambition has slept in our limits
  Since fearless Columbia sheathed her bright blade:
And at her dread Vengeance on those who awake it,
  The soul of the stoutest might well be dismayed.

Beware! for the spirit of God's Retribution
  Will make a red sunrise when Liberty dies;
The Traitors shall writhe in the glow of a morning,
  And drown in the blood that is filling their eyes!

The bright blade of old, when it leaps from the scabbard
  Like Lightning shall fall on the traitorous head,
And hurl with each stroke, in its world-shock of thunder,
  A thrice cursed soul to the deeps of the Dead!

Beware ! for when once ye have made your Red Ocean,
  Its waves shall rise up with tempestuous swell,
And hurl your stained souls, like impurities, from them
  Up death's dark slope, to the skull beach of Hell !

KARAZAH TO KARL.

COME back to me ! my life is young,
　　My soul is scarcely on her way,
And all the starry songs she's sung,
　　Are prelude to a grander lay.
　　　　　　　Come back to me !

Let this song-born soul receive thee,
　　Glowing its fondest truth to prove ;
Why so early did'st thou leave me,
　　Are our heaven-grand life of love ?
　　　　　　　Come back to me !

My burning lips shall set their seal
　　On our betrothal bond to-night,
While whispering murmurs will reveal
　　How souls can love in God's own light.
　　　　　　　Come back to me !

Come back to me !　The stars will be
　　Silent witnesses of our bliss,
And all the past shall seem to thee
　　But a sweet dream to herald this !
　　　　　　　Come back to me !

A FRAGMENT.

"Oh! I am sick of what I am.   Of all
Which I in life can ever hope to be.
Angels of light be pitiful to me."

THE cold chain of life presseth heavily on me to-
night.

The thundering pace of thought is curbed, and, like a
fiery steed, dasheth against the gloomy walls of my prisoned soul.

Oh! how long will my poor thoughts lament their narrow faculty?   When will the rein be loosed from my impatient soul?

Ah! then I will climb the blue clouds and dash down
to dust those jeweled stars, whose silent light wafts a
mocking laugh to the poor musician who sitteth before
the muffled organ of my great hopes.   With a hand of
fire he toucheth the golden keys.   All breathless and rapt
I list for an answer to his sweet meaning, but the glittering keys give back only a faint hollow sound—the echo of
a sigh!

Cruel stars to mock me with your laughing light!

Oh! see ye not the purple life-blood ebbing from my
side?

But ye heed it not—and I scorn ye all.

48

Foolish stars! Ye forget that this strong soul will one day be loosed.

I will have ye in my power yet, I'll meet ye on the grand door of old eternity.

Ah! then ye will not laugh, but shrink before me like very beggars of light that ye are, and I will grasp from your gleaming brows the jeweled crown, rend away your glistening garments, and hold ye up blackened skeletons for the laugh and scorn of all angels, and then drive ye out to fill this horrid space of darkness that I now grovel in.

But, alas! I am weary, sick, and faint.

The chains do bind the shrinking flesh too close.

> "Angels of light, be pitiful to me."

Oh! this life, after all, is but a promise—a poor promise, that is too heavy to bear—heavy with blood, reeking human blood. The atmosphere is laden with it. When I shut my eyes it presses so close to their lids that I must gasp and struggle to open them.

I know that the sins of untrue hearts are clogging up the air-passages of the world, and that we, who love and suffer, will soon be smothered, and in this terrible darkness too.

For me—my poor lone, deserted body—I care not. I am not in favor of men's eyes.

> "Nor am I skilled immortal stuff to weave.
> No rose of honor wear I on my sleeve."

But the soft silver hand of death will unbind the galling

bands that clasp the fretting soul in her narrow prison-house, and she may then escape the iron hands that would crush the delicate fibres to dust.

O soul, where are thy wings? Have they with their rude hands torn them from thy mutilated form? We must creep slowly and silently away through the midnight darkness. But we are strong yet, and can battle with the fiends who seek to drive us back to the river of blood.

But, alas! it is so late, and I am alone—alone listening to the gasps and sighs of a weary soul beating her broken wing against the darkened walls of her lonely cell.

> "My labor is a vain and empty strife,
>   A useless tugging at the wheels of life."

Shall I still live—filling no heart, working no good, and the cries of my holy down-trodden race haunting me? Beseeching me—me, with these frail arms and this poor chained soul, to lift them back to their birthright of glory.

> "Angels of light, be pitiful to me."

I have wearied Heaven with my tears and prayers till I have grown pale and old, but a shadow of my former self, and all for power, blessed power! Not for myself—but for those dearer and worthier than I—those from out whose hearts my memory has died for ever.

But, alas! it is vain.

Prayers and tears will not bring back sweet hope and love.

I may still sigh and weep for these soft winged nestling

angels of my lost dreams till I am free to seek them in the grand homes where I have housed them with the golden-haired son of the sky.

It is midnight, and the world is still battling—the weak are falling, the strong and the wrong are exulting.

And I, like the dying stag, am hunted down to the ocean border, still asking for peace and rest of the great gleaming eyes that pierce the atmosphere of blood and haunt me with their pleading looks. Whispers are there —low, wailing whispers from white-browed children as though I could bear their chained souls o'er Charon's mystic river of their purple blood.

Alas! star after star has gone down till not one is in sight. How dark and cold it is growing!

Oh, light! why have you fled to a fairer land and left

> " An unrigged hulk, to rot upon life's ford—
> The crew of mutinous senses overboard?"

It is too late. I faint with fear of these atom-fiends that do cling to my garments in this darkness.

> Oh! rest for thee, my weary soul,
>   The coil is round thee all too fast.
> Too close to earth thy pinions clasp:
>   A trance-like death hath o'er thee past.

> Oh, soul! oh, broken soul, arise,
>   And plume thee for a prouder flight.
> In vain, in vain—'tis sinking now
>   And dying in eternal night.

> " Suffer and be still."

Death will bind up thy powerful wings, and to the organ music of my great hopes thou shalt beat sublimer airs.

Wait until eternity.

THE AUTOGRAPH ON THE SOUL.

IN the Beginning, God, the great Schoolmaster, wrote upon the white leaves of our souls the text of life, in His own autograph.

Upon all souls it has been written alike.

We set forth with the broad, fair characters penned in smoothness and beauty, and promise to bear them back so, to the Master, who will endorse them with eternal life.

But, alas ! how few of us can return with these copybooks unstained and unblotted ?

Man—the school-boy Man—takes a jagged pen and dips it in blood, and scrawls line after line of his hopeless, shaky, weak-backed, spattering imitation of the unattainable flourish and vigor of the autograph at the top of our souls.

And thus they go on, in unweary reiteration, until the fair leaves are covered with unseemly blots, and the Schoolmaster's copy is no longer visible.

No wonder, then, that we shrink and hide, and play truant as long as we possibly can, before handing in to the Master our copy-books for examination.

How soiled with the dust of men, and stained with the blood of the innocent, some of these books are !

Surely, some will look fairer than others.

Those of the lowly and despised of men ;
The wronged and the persecuted ;
The loving and the deserted ;
The suffering and the despairing ;
The weak and the struggling ;
The desolate and the oppressed ;
The authors of good books ;
The defenders of women ;
The mothers of new-born children ;
The loving wives of cruel husbands ;
The strong throats that are choked with their own blood, and cannot cry out the oppressor's wrong.

On the souls of these of God's children of inspiration, His autograph will be handed up to the judgment-seat, on the Day of Examination, pure and unsoiled.

The leaf may be torn, and traces of tears, that fell as prayers went up, may dim the hòly copy, but its fair, sharp, and delicate outlines will only gleam the stronger, and prove the lesson of life, that poor, down-trodden humanity has been studying for ages and ages—the eternal triumph of mind over matter !

What grand poems these starving souls will be, after they are signed and sealed by the Master-hand !

But what of the oppressor ?

What of the betrayer ?

What of him that holds a deadly cup, that the pure of heart may drink ?

What of fallen women, who are covered with paint and sin, and flaunt in gaudy satins, never heeding the black stains within their own breasts ?—lost to honor, lost to themselves ; glittering in jewels and gold ; mingling with sinful men, who, with sneering looks and scoffing laughs, drink wine beneath the gas-light's glare.

Wrecks of womanly honor !

Wrecks of womanly souls !

Wrecks of life and love !

Blots that deface the fair earth with crime and sin !

Fallen—fallen so low that the cries and groans of the damned must sometimes startle their death-signed hearts, as they flaunt through the world, with God's curse upon them !

What of the money-makers, with their scorching days and icy nights ?

Their hollow words and ghastly smiles ?

Their trifling deceits ?

Their shameless lives ?

Their starving menials ?

Their iron hands, that grasp the throats of weary, white-haired men ?

Will their coffins be black ?

They should be red—stained with the blood of their victims !

Their shrouds should be make with pockets ; and all their gold should be placed therein, to drag them deeper down than the sexton dug the grave !

How will it be with him who deceives and betrays women ?

Answer me this, ye men who have brought woe and desolation to the heart of woman ; and, by your fond lips, breathing sighs, and vows of truth and constancy—your deceit and desertion, destroyed her, body and soul !

There are more roads to the heart than by cold steel.

You drew her life and soul after you by your pretended love.   Perhaps she sacrificed her home, her father and her mother—her God and her religion for you !

Perhaps for you she has endured pain and penury !

Perhaps she is the mother of your child, living and praying for you !

And how do you repay this devotion ?

By entering the Eden of her soul, and leaving the trail of the serpent, that can never be erased from its flowers ; for the best you trample beneath your feet, while the fairest you pluck as a toy to while away an idle hour, then dash aside for another of a fairer cast.

Then, if she plead with her tears, and her pure hands, to Heaven, that you come back to your lost honor, and to her heart, you do not hesitate to tear that suffering heart with a shameless word, that cuts like a jagged knife, and add your curse to crush her light of life !

Have ye seen the blood-stained steel, dimmed with the heart's warm blood of the suicide ?

Have ye seen the pallid lips, the staring eyes, the un- closed, red-roofed mouth—the bubbling gore, welling up from a woman's breast ?

Have ye seen her dying in shivering dread, with the blood dabbled o'er her bosom ?

Have ye heard her choked voice rise in prayer—her pale lips breathing his name—the name of him who de- ceived her ?   Yes ! a prayer coming up with the bubbling blood—a blessing on him for whom she died !

Why did she not pray for her despairing self ?

O God ! have mercy on the souls of men who are false to their earthly love and trust !

But the interest will come round—all will come round!
Nothing will escape the Schoolmaster's sleepless eye!
The indirect is always as great and real as the direct.

Not one word or deed—
Not one look or thought—

Not a motive but will be stamped on the programme of
our lives, and duly realized by us, and returned and held
up to light heaven or flood hell with.

All the best actions of war or peace—
All the help given to strangers—
Cheering words to the despairing—
Open hands to the shunned—
Lifting of lowly hearts—
Teaching children of God—
Helping the widow and the fatherless—
Giving light to some desolate home—
Reading the Bible to the blind—
Protecting the defenceless—
Praying with the dying.

These are acts that need no Poet to make poems of
them; for they will live through ages and ages, on to
Eternity. And when God opens the sealed book on the
Day of Judgment, these poems of the history of lives will
be traced in letters of purple and gold, beneath the Master's Autograph.

ADELINA PATTI.

THOU Pleiad of the lyric world
    Where Pasta, Garcia shone,
Come back with thy sweet voice again,
    And gem the starry zone.

Though faded, still the vision sees
    The loveliest child of night,
The fairest of the Pleiades,
    Its glory and its light.

How fell with music from thy tongue
    The picture which it drew
Of Lucia, radiant, warm, and young—
    Amina, fond and true.

Or the young Marie's grace and art,
    So free from earthly strife,
Beating upon the sounding heart,
    The gay tattoo of life!

Fair Florence! home of glorious Art,
    And mistress of its sphere,
Clasp fast thy beauties to thy heart—
    Behold thy rival here!

DYING.

I.

LEAVE me; oh! leave me,
  Lest I find this low earth sweeter than the skies.
  Leave me lest I deem Faith's white bosom bared to
the betraying arms of Death.
  Hush your fond voice, lest it shut out the angel trum-
pet-call!
  See my o'erwearied feet bleed for rest.
  Loose the clinging and the clasping of my clammy
fingers.
  Your soft hand of Love may press back the dark,
awful shadows of Death, but the soul faints in the strife
and struggles of nights that have no days.
  I am so weary with this climbing up the smooth steep
sides of the grave wall.
  My dimmed eyes can no longer strain up through the
darkness to the temples and palaces that you have built
for me upon Life's summit.
  God is folding up the white tent of my youth.
  My name is enrolled for the pallid army of the dead.

II.

  It is too late, too late!
  You may not kiss back my breath to the sunshine.

How can these trembling hands of dust reach up to bend the untempered iron of Destiny down to my woman-forehead?

Where is the wedge to split its knotty way between the Past and the Future?

The soaring bird that would sing its life out to the stars, may not leave its own atmosphere;

For, in the long dead reaches of blank space in the Beyond, its free wings fall back to earth baffled.

Once gathering all my sorrows up to one purpose—rebel-like—I dared step out into Light, when, lo! Death tied my unwilling feet, and with hands of ice, bandaged my burning lips, and set up, between my eyes and the Future, the great Infinite of Eternity, full in the blazing sun of my Hope!

From the red round life of Love I have gone down to the naked house of Fear.

Drowned in a storm of tears.

My wild wings of thought drenched from beauty to the color of the ground.

Going out at the hueless gates of day.

Dying, dying.

III.

Oh! is there no strength in sorrow, or in prayers?

Is there no power in the untried wings of the soul, to smite the brazen portals of the sun?

Must the black-sandaled foot of Night tramp out the one star that throbs through the darkness of my waning life?

May not the strong arm of "I will," bring some beam to lead me into my sweet Hope again?

Alas, too late! too late!

The power of these blood-dripping cerements sweeps back the audacious thought to emptiness.

Hungry Death will not heed the poor bird that has tangled its bright wing through my deep-heart pulses.

> Moaning and living.
> Dying and loving.

IV.

See the poor wounded snake; how burdened to the ground;

How it lengthens limberly along the dust.

Now palpitates into bright rings only to unwind, and reach its bleeding head up the steep high walls around us.

Now, alas! falling heavily back into itself, quivering with unuttered pain;

Choking with its own blood it dies in the dust.

> So we are crippled ever;
> Reaching and falling,
> Silent and dying.

V.

Gold and gleaming jewel shatter off their glory well in the robes of royalty, but when we strain against the whelming waves, the water gurgling down our drowning throats, we shred them off, and hug the wet, cold rocks lovingly.

Then old death goes moaning back from the steady footing of Life baffled.

Ah! is it too late for me to be wise.

Will my feeble hands fail me in the moveless steppings back to the world?

Oh! if youth were only back!

Oh! if the years would only empty back their ruined days into the lap of the Present!

Oh! if yesterday would only unravel the light it wove into the purple of the Past!

Ah! then might I be vigilant!

Then might the battle be mine!

Nor should my sluggish blood drip down the rocks till the noon-tide sun should draw it up mistily in smoke.

Then should the heaviness of soul have dropped as trees do their weight of rainy leaves.

Nor should the sweet leash of Love have slipped from my hungry life, and left me pining, dying for his strength.

I should have wrapt up my breathing in the naked bosom of Nature, and she would have kissed me back to sweetest comfort, and I would have drawn up from her heart draughts of crusted nectar and promises of eternal joys.

Oh! it is not the glittering garniture of God's things that come quivering into the senses, that makes our lives look white through the windings of the wilderness.

It is the soul's outflow of purple light that clashes up a music with the golden blood of strong hearts.

Souls with God's breath upon them,
Hearts with Love's light upon them.

VI.

If my weak puny hand could reach up and rend the sun

from his throne to-day, then were the same but a little thing for me to do.

It is the Far Off, the great Unattainable, that feeds the passion we feel for a star.

Looking up so high, worshiping so silently, we tramp out the hearts of flowers that lift their bright heads for us and die alone.

If only the black, steep grave gaped between us, I feel that I could over-sweep all its gulfs.

I believe that Love may unfold its white wings even in the red bosom of Hell.

I know that its truth can measure the distance to Heaven with one thought.

Then be content to let me go, for these pale hands shall reach up from the grave, and still draw the living waters of Love's well.

That is better, surer than climbing with bruised feet and bleeding hands to plead with the world for what is mine own.

Then straighten out the crumpled length of my hair, and loose all the flowers one by one.

God is not unjust.

VII.

Oh! in the great strength of thy unhooded soul, pray for my weakness.

Let me go! See the pale and solemn army of the night is on the march.

Do not let my shivering soul go wailing up for a human love to the throne of the Eternal.

Have we not watched the large setting sun drive a

column of light through the horizon down into the darkness?

So within the grave's night, O my beloved! shall my love burn on to eternity.

O Death! Death! loose out thy cold, stiff fingers from my quivering heart!

Let the warm blood rush back to gasp up but one more word!

O Love! thou art stronger, mightier than all!

O Death! thou hast but wedded me to Life!

Life is Love, and Love is Eternity.

SAVED.

I.

O SOLDIERS, soldiers, get ye back, I pray!
  Hush out of sound your trampings so near his
lowly head!
  Hush back the echoes of your footfalls to the muffling
distance!
  O soldiers, wake not my sleeping love!
  Get ye back, I pray!
  To-morrow will he wake, and lead ye on as bravely as
before.
  To-morrow will he lift the blazing sword above a crim-
son flood of victory.
  Get ye back and wait.
  He is weary, and would sleep.

II.

  Soft, soft, he sleepeth well.
  Why stand ye all so stern and sad?
  So garmented in the dust and blood of battle?
  Why linger on the field to-day? See how the dark
locks hang in bloody tangles about your glaring eyes!
  Get ye to your silent tents, I pray!
  See ye not your soldier-chief sleeps safe and well?

What say ye?

"Dead!"

O blind, blind soldiers! Should I not know?

Have I not watched him all the long, long battle?

On this cold and sunless plain my tottering feet struck the pathway to my soldier.

My loving arms have clasped him from the black, hungry jaws of Death.

With the neglected sunshine of my hair I shielded his pale face from the cannon-glare.

On my breast, as on a wave of heaven-light, have I lulled him to the soft beauty of dreams.

He has been yours to-day; he is mine now.

He has fought bravely, and would sleep.

I know, I know.

III.

O soldiers, soldiers, take him not hence!

Do not press tears back into your pitiful eyes, and say : " His soul hath found its rest."

Why lean ye on your blood-stained spears, and point to that dark wound upon his throat?

I can kiss its pain and terror out.

Leave him, I pray ye!

He will wake to-morrow, and cheer ye in your tents at dawn.

And ye shall see him smile on her who soothes his weary head to sleep through this long night.

It was I who found him at the battle's dreadful close.

Weary and wounded, he sank to rest upon the field.

Murmuring out his tender voice, he called my name, and whispered of our love, and its sweet eternity.

'Mid brooding love and clinging kisses, his tender eyes let down their silken barriers to the day.

Their pale roofs close out the defeat, and in my arms he finds the joy of glorious victory.

IV.

O soldiers, leave him to me !

The morning, bridegroomed by the sun, cannot look down to the midnight for comfort.

In the thick front of battle I claimed what is mine own.

I saw the Grim Foe open wide his red-leafed book, but he wrote not therein the name of my brave love.

Life hath no chance that he cannot combat with a single hand.

Now he wearies from the struggling grace of a brave surrendering.

He sleeps, he sleeps.

Go, soldiers, go !

I pray ye wake him not.

I have kissed his pale, cold mouth, and staunched the crimson wound upon his throat.

The mournful moon has seen my silent watch above his lonely bed.

Her pitying eyes reproached me not.

How durst yours ?

Go, soldiers, go !

VI.

I charge ye by the love ye bear your sleeping chieftain, wake him not !

To-morrow he will wake, eager to wheel into battle-line.

To-morrow he will rise, and mount the steed he loveth well, and lead ye cheerily on to the attack !

To-morrow his voice will ring its Hope along your tramping troops !

But oh ! wait, wait !

He is weary, and must sleep !

Go, soldiers, go !

ANSWER ME.

I.

IN from the night.
    The storm is lifting his black arms up to the sky.
Friend of my heart, who so gently marks out the life-track for me, draw near to-night;
Forget the wailing of the low-voiced wind:
Shut out the moanings of the freezing, and the starving, and the dying, and bend your head low to me:
Clasp my cold, cold hands in yours;
Think of me tenderly and lovingly:
Look down into my eyes thé while I question you, and if you love me, answer me—
              Oh, answer me!

II.

Is there not a gleam of Peace on all this tiresome earth?
Does not one oasis cheer all this desert-world?
When will all this toil and pain bring me the blessing?
Must I ever plead for help to do the work before me set?
Must I ever stumble and faint by the dark wayside?
Oh the dark, lonely wayside, with its dim-sheeted ghosts peering up through their shallow graves!

Must I ever tremble and pale at the great Beyond?
Must I find Rest only in your bosom, as now I do?
                    Answer me—
                    Oh, answer me!

III.

Speak to me tenderly.

Think of me lovingly.

Let your soft hands smooth back my hair.

Take my cold, tear-stained face up to yours.

Let my lonely life creep into your warm bosom, know·
ing no other rest but this.

Let me question you, while sweet Faith and Trust are
folding their white robes around me.

Thus am I purified, even to your love, that came like
John the Baptist in the Wilderness of Sin.

You read the starry heavens, and lead me forth.

But tell me if, in this world's Judea, there comes never
quiet when once the heart awakes?

Why must it ever hush Love back?

Must it only labor, strive, and ache?

Has it no reward but this?

Has it no inheritance but to bear—and break?
                    Answer me—
                    Oh, answer me!

IV.

The Storm struggles with the Darkness.

Folded away in your arms, how little do I heed their
battle!

The trees clash in vain their naked swords against the door.

I go not forth while the low murmur of your voice is drifting all else back to silence.

The darkness presses his black forehead close to the window pane, and beckons me without.

Love holds a lamp in this little room that hath power to blot back Fear.

But will the lamp ever starve for oil?

Will its blood-red flame ever grow faint and blue?

Will it uprear itself to a slender line of light?

Will it grow pallid and motionless?

Will it sink rayless to everlasting death?

Answer me—

Oh, answer me!

V.

Look at these tear-drops.

See how they quiver and die on your open hands.

Fold these white garments close to my breast, while I question you.

Would you have me think that from the warm shelter of your heart I must go to the grave?

And when I am lying in my silent shroud, will you love me?

When I am buried down in the cold, wet earth, will you grieve that you did not save me?

Will your tears reach my pale face through all the withered leaves that will heap themselves upon my grave?

Will you repent that you loosened your arms to let me fall so deep, and so far out of sight?

Will you come and tell me so, when the coffin has shut
out the storm?

            Answer me—
            Oh, answer me !

INFELIX.

WHERE is the promise of my years;
    Once written on my brow?
Ere errors, agonies and fears
Brought with them all that speaks in tears,
Ere I had sunk beneath my peers;
    Where sleeps that promise now?

Naught lingers to redeem those hours,
    Still, still to memory sweet!
The flowers that bloomed in sunny bowers
Are withered all; and Evil towers
Supreme above her sister powers
    Of Sorrow and Deceit.

I look along the columned years,
    And see Life's riven fane,
Just where it fell, amid the jeers
Of scornful lips, whose mocking sneers,
For ever hiss within mine ears
    To break the sleep of pain.

I can but own my life is vain
    A desert void of peace;

I missed the goal I sought to gain,
I missed the measure of the strain
That lulls Fame's fever in the brain,
    And bids Earth's tumult cease.

Myself! alas for theme so poor
    A theme but rich in Fear;
I stand a wreck on Error's shore,
A spectre not within the door,
A houseless shadow evermore,
    An exile lingering here.